The Quakers: A Very Short Introduction

VERY SHORT INTRODUCTIONS are for anyone wanting
a stimulating and accessible way in to a new subject. They are
written by experts and have been translated into more than
40 different languages. The series began in 1995 and now covers
a wide variety of topics in every discipline. The VSI library contains
nearly 400 volumes—a Very Short Introduction to everything
from Indian philosophy to psychology and American history—and
continues to grow in every subject area.

Very Short Introductions available now:

Pink Dandelion

THE QUAKERS

A Very Short Introduction

OXFORD
UNIVERSITY PRESS

Great Clarendon Street, Oxford OX2 6DP

Oxford University Press is a department of the University of Oxford.
It furthers the University's objective of excellence in research, scholarship,
and education by publishing worldwide in

Oxford New York

Auckland Cape Town Dar es Salaam Hong Kong Karachi
Kuala Lumpur Madrid Melbourne Mexico City Nairobi
New Delhi Shanghai Taipei Toronto

With offices in

Argentina Austria Brazil Chile Czech Republic France Greece
Guatemala Hungary Italy Japan Poland Portugal Singapore
South Korea Switzerland Thailand Turkey Ukraine Vietnam

Oxford is a registered trade mark of Oxford University Press
in the UK and in certain other countries

Published in the United States
by Oxford University Press Inc., New York

British Library Cataloguing in Publication Data

Data available

Library of Congress Cataloging in Publication Data

Data available

ISBN 978-0-19-920679-7

9 10

Typeset by SPI Publisher Services, Pondicherry, India
Printed in Great Britain by
Ashford Colour Press Ltd, Gosport, Hampshire

For Wendy and Florence

Contents

List of illustrations

Chapter 1
Who are the Quakers?

It is often said that the Quakers have had an influence beyond their numbers. Certainly, through their class and educational background, Quakers have had an important role in the formation of civil society on both sides of the Atlantic. Quaker opposition to war and work for peace, as well as the social witness which emerged out of their idea of spiritual equality, such as Elizabeth Fry's prison work or the opposition to slavery, is perhaps what Quakers are best known for today. People may know that some of them worship in silence or that they don't have priests, but it is their public witness that has given them the most prominence. At the same time, they are theologically and sociologically fascinating, beginning as a radical movement during the British republic, and adapting themselves forever thereafter to new theological insights and new social settings. This book outlines the movement and its history, charts how different traditions of Quakers worship, and explores what they believe. It looks at Quaker attitudes to other Churches and other faiths, and considers the future of Quakerism.

The Quakers began as a movement in the northwest of England in 1652, although, as we shall see, some of the key experiences of the early Friends (as Quakers are also called) occurred some years previously. Through mission and migration, there are now around 340,000 Quakers worldwide. Through the kind of schism that seems to categorize sectarian Protestantism, there are three main traditions of Quakerism: Evangelical (although there are also different varieties of Evangelical Friend), Conservative, and Liberal. Nevertheless, there are four key theological ideas still held in common by Friends everywhere:

1) the centrality of direct inward encounter with God and revelation, and thus forms of worship which allow this to be experienced: 'Quaker' was originally a nickname applied to the group because of the way they shook during worship;

2) a vote-less way of doing church business based on the idea of corporate direct guidance;

3) the spiritual equality of everyone and the idea of 'the priesthood of all believers';

4) based in part on the latter, the preference for peace and pacifism rather than war, and a commitment to other forms of social witness.

This chapter gives an overview of the founding ideas of the movement, charts the centrality of witness or 'testimony' to the movement and to how the movement has come to be known, and briefly delineates the different types of Quaker.

Beginnings

George Fox (1624–91) is generally credited with the founding of the Quaker movement, although he came to be helped by a great number of very capable preachers such as James Nayler, Margaret Fell, Edward Burrough, Francis Howgill, Richard Hubberthorne, Richard Farnsworth, and William Dewsbury, all drawn initially from the north of England. Fox himself grew up in Fenny Drayton in Leicestershire. His religious seeking led him to leave home in 1643 when he was 19 years of age and he spent the next few years

GEORGE FOX.

Founder of the Society of Friends, usually called Quakers.

1. Wood engraving of George Fox (1624–91)

with a Baptist uncle in London and visiting the army camps. This was the Civil War period, and it was in the Parliamentary army that the most radical religious ideas were circulating.

Fox had already realized that the national Church's notion that ministers needed to be educated at Oxford or Cambridge was

wrongheaded, but he also found the radical preachers who had
separated from the Church lacking. We see this reflected in the
following passage from his journal, dated 1647, but we also read of
the transforming experience that came over him in the depths of
his despair.

> Now after I had received that opening from the Lord that to be
> bred at Oxford or Cambridge was not sufficient to fit a man to be a
> minister of Christ, I regarded the priests less and looked more after
> the dissenting people ... [But] As I had forsaken all the priests,
> so I left the separate preachers also, and those called the most
> experienced people; for I saw there was none among them all that
> could speak to my condition. And when all my hopes in them and
> in all men were gone, so that I had nothing *outwardly* to help me,
> nor could tell what to do, then, oh then, I heard a voice which said,
> 'There is one, even Christ Jesus, that can speak to thy condition',
> and when I heard it my heart did leap for joy.
>
> (Nickalls, 1952, p. 11; my emphasis)

In other words, at the very point when Fox had no hope and knew
not where to turn, he claims this direct experience of God and
Christ speaking to him. He continues:

> Then the Lord did let me see why there was none upon the earth
> that could speak to my condition, namely, that I might give him all
> the glory; for all are concluded under sin, and shut up in unbelief
> as I had been, that Jesus Christ might have the preeminence
> who enlightens, and gives grace, and faith, and power. Thus,
> when God doth work who shall let [hinder] it? And this I knew
> experimentally.
>
> (Nickalls, 1952, p. 11)

The important point about this passage is that Fox realizes that
it is no accident that he has not found easy answers from those

around him. Wisdom and guidance is to come from God and those who think otherwise are 'shut up in unbelief', deluded. He knows this 'experimentally', that is, through his experience.

This experience was and remains foundational for Quakerism. In the next chapter, we shall see how its interpretation shifted over time and between Quaker traditions, but the idea and experience of direct encounter remains central for all kinds of Quaker today.

Critically, for Fox, the importance he gave revelation was not additional to Church teaching and the authority of scripture, but replaced it. 'How do we know what is of God?' is a key question for all religious groups. Fox claimed that direct revelation was the answer. Equally importantly, he claimed this revelation was available to everyone; it wasn't that he had a particular spiritual authority but that he had discovered the authority available for everyone.

Fox claimed that the revelation given to him was always later confirmed by scripture but that scripture was secondary to revelation, it was the word about the Living Word, the inward experience of Christ. Early Friends used Jeremiah 31: 31–34 to affirm this experience of a new covenant with God written on their hearts, rather than in outward forms.

Indeed, Quaker spirituality placed great emphasis on the authenticity of the inward and the apostasy (the falling away from the faith) of the outward. This transforming experience available to all did away with the need for priests and sermons, for the Teacher spoke inwardly and directly.

A year later, in 1648, Fox had a second experience during which he felt himself lifted up into the state of Adam before the Fall, but then quickly into a state beyond Adam, beyond falling.

Now I was come up in spirit through the flaming sword into the paradise of God. All things were new, and all creation gave another smell unto me than before, beyond what words can utter. I knew nothing but pureness, and innocency, and righteousness, being renewed up into the image of God by Christ Jesus, so that I say I was come up to the state of Adam which he was in before he fell ... But I was immediately taken up in spirit to see into another or more steadfast state than Adam's in innocency, even into a state in Christ Jesus that should never fall.

(Nickalls, 1952, p. 27)

The 'flaming sword' is a reference to Genesis 3 in which a flaming sword is placed across the entrance to Eden once Adam and Eve have been banished. What Fox is claiming here is a spiritual intimacy with God and Christ, entailing an ability to resist sin and temptation, that is, a doctrine of perfection. This spiritual intimacy and the transformation it brought gave Friends a sense of being on a new and separated spiritual plane from their old selves and from the rest of humanity. They called themselves 'the saints' or 'the Friends of the Truth', and felt themselves separate from the apostate 'world'. In some early Quaker tracts, they claimed their names belonged only to their former lives, that they were now 'truly known' only by the other saints and by God.

The transformation experience that Quakers underwent, or 'convincement' as it came to be termed, consisted of six stages for most Friends:

1) an in-breaking of God's power;
2) a realization of how sinful the believer's life had been, how far it had fallen short;
3) the chance to repent and accept the new life;
4) the experience of regeneration;
5) an impulse to gather with others who had had this experience;
6) mission to those who had not yet had this experience.

Early Friends also claimed the experience of transformation was continual. It is not clear how many claimed the perfection Fox did, but it was certainly a recognized Quaker doctrine through the 1650s.

Following his 1647 and 1648 experiences, Fox stayed in the Midlands but spent most of 1650 in jail, a common experience for Quakers in the first 30 years of the movement. When he was released, he travelled north to where groups of 'Seekers' were already sharing some of his ideas. The Seekers were a group who had separated away from the national Church and had stripped their worship of formal liturgy. They had ministers but met in silence until the minister spoke. There were strong groups of Seekers in Yorkshire and Westmoreland, and much of the early Quaker leadership was drawn from their numbers. Edward Burrough was one of the Westmoreland Seekers who became a leading Quaker, but in 1656 wrote a tract against the Seekers for merely 'waiting'. In other words, from this publication, we have a sense that the Seekers perhaps lacked a vision or a vehicle to take the next steps towards the coming of the Kingdom. For many of them, George Fox seemed to fulfil that function.

Travelling from Yorkshire to Westmoreland in May 1652, Fox felt 'moved by the Lord' to climb Pendle Hill, near Clitheroe in Lancashire. At the top and on the way down, Fox had a vision of a 'great people to be gathered, dressed in white raiment' (another reference to Revelation) (Nickalls, 1952, p. 104). This was a critical moment in Quaker history as it marked the idea of starting the new Church rather than just preaching truth. Two weeks later he arrived in Sedbergh, at the time of the hiring fair for flax workers, who dressed in white, and the following Sunday afternoon on Firbank Fell, where there was a Seeker meeting in the morning, Fox 'drew many hundreds to land'. In other words, he had a major preaching success which began the Quaker movement more formally. Two weeks after that, in Ulverston, he converted Margaret Fell, part of the local gentry, and her household at Swarthmoor Hall, to the Quaker experience, and secured in Fell the co-leadership of the movement in the early years and huge pastoral, administrative, and theological skills, as well as the protection of her husband, Judge Thomas Fell. Swarthmoor Hall became the headquarters of the Quaker movement for the next few years. In 1654, the mission to the rest of England and Wales, and later to Ireland, the Vatican and Constantinople, and the Americas, left from there.

Quakerism in context

In some ways, we can say that the Quaker movement began in the 1650s in response to two aspects of Christian history: first, the Protestant impulse to more fully reform Christianity; and second, the waiting for the Second Coming upon which Christianity as a formal religion is founded.

Since the Reformation of 1534, when Henry VIII had set up a national Church separate from the Roman Catholic one, some had wished his reforms to go further. His reformation was more political than theological and left many radical thinkers frustrated. The availability of the Bible in English after 1590, and especially after 1611 when an English-language Bible could be found in every church, fuelled the desire for fresh interpretations of liturgical form and ecclesiology (the way the Church is structured). The Civil War period gave new momentum to the discussion of radical religious ideas and a new sense of possibility. The moderate religious settlement that characterized the 1650s and rule under Oliver Cromwell frustrated many, but also gave enough freedom to sectarian groups to allow the Quakers to present themselves as the new true Church, the model of a fully reformed Church.

Christianity itself emerged as a religion as the early Christians came to realize that the Second Coming of Christ, prophesied by Paul, was not necessarily going to take place immediately.

Humanity needed help to wait faithfully and the institution of the Church and its officers and practices was a pragmatic response to that need. Official Church documents are explicit about the temporary nature of these rites and institutions. Visit an Anglican or Roman Catholic church today and you find the liturgy of the Eucharist is explicitly about the remembrance of the First Coming and the anticipation of the Second. As the theologian Albert Schweitzer commented, the history of Christianity has been about the delay of the Second Coming.

Early Quakers felt they were in the vanguard of this Second Coming which would come to all and bring about global transformation. Again, building on Jeremiah, but also Revelation in particular, these early Friends claimed that this Second Coming was an inward experience. This new reality available to all meant that the way Christianity had been operating was now redundant and anachronistic, belonging only to an age now past.

Thus, as well as not needing priests and sermons, this interpretation of the direct encounter between humanity and God, and the continual nature of the transformation it brought, also meant that churches and outward sacraments could be dispensed with. Revelation 3:20 talks about Christ supping inwardly with those who respond to his knocking, and Friends thought this communion replaced the passage in 1 Corinthians 11:26 that instructs the believers to break the bread until the Lord comes. The Lord had come again. There was a new supper to celebrate, the marriage supper of the Lamb. Equally, the Church calendar set up to help remember and anticipate could be ignored. Every day was equally holy and special. Neither Sunday nor Christmas or Easter was marked by these early Friends. Every place was equally holy given the continual and personal nature of transformation, and Quakers met to preach and worship anywhere: often in barns or by the roadside. The Quakers built 'Meeting Houses' only when their own homes became too small.

2. A Quaker Meeting from the 17th century

Quakers thus presented themselves as the end of waiting, both
for full reformation, but also, in the much bigger picture, for
the unfolding Second Coming. 'Christ is come and is Coming'
they claimed. Christ had come to those who had experienced
'convincement' and would come to all. Quakers were the true
Church, God's elect and God's vanguard, but all could be part
of the elect and attain salvation; all were spiritually equal. This
infuriated Calvinist thinkers with their doctrine of predestination,
as did the apparent arrogance of most of the claims upon which
the Quakers based their movement.

Quakers and their Meetings

The early Friends adopted silence as the medium through which
to experience God's revelation. Meetings would typically last
three hours, could take place anywhere, and were characterized

by large amounts of preaching interspersed by silence rather than the other way round. There is evidence of worshippers groaning and moaning in approval of what was spoken. Those offering 'ministry' would stand. Prayer, however, would involve the speaker kneeling and everyone else standing and removing their hats, the only time Quakers did so. Given the idea of spiritual equality, anyone could speak when prompted by God. Indeed, the ministry of women, who made up 45% of the early Quaker movement, was significant for its time, and critical to the success of Quakerism. As well as these meetings of the saints, there would be public preaching meetings and threshing meetings where ideas would be debated amongst the more interested. Quakers also performed signs, such as 'going naked', as part of their public witness to the new covenant they had established with God and the apostasy of the old ways of believing. Worship is considered more fully in Chapter 3.

Business practice within this new Church and the structure of the Church evolved more slowly but necessarily accommodated the idea that God spoke to the Church, that is, the body of believers, directly. This was where authority lay and silence was again used as the medium through which God's guidance could be heard. Quakers became fastidious record-keepers, making minutes of the decisions they reached within the Meetings so that they could be agreed by everyone present.

The new Church was generally decentralized, with local groups making decisions for themselves, but an extensive correspondence between Quakers and the itinerance of key leaders ensured uniformity of practice and belief. Only in the 1660s did the structure centralize.

Leadership was informal and there was no fixed hierarchy of spiritual authority, although Elders emerged as a functional role quite early on. When Fox died in 1691, there was no vacuum of leadership: it was already being shared.

Quaker witness and testimony

As well as radical consequences for worship and business, the experience of early Friends led to a whole range of ways of behaving in the world and amongst the world's people.

They refused to pay church tithes which were used to fund the upkeep of 'mashouses' or 'steeplehouses' and 'hireling ministers', as they called them, and once in court for this offence or any of the many other laws they fell foul of, they would refuse to swear on oath. In Matthew, it says to 'swear not at all', and Quakers felt it implied a double-standard to swear to tell the truth in court when they claimed they maintained honesty and integrity at all times. Exchanges in court over Quaker witness or testimony were often turned into preaching opportunities by these early Friends.

The Quakers also preferred to use numbers for days and months rather than the pagan names, so they would call Sunday first day, Monday second day, and so on, and the months would be numbered also. When the calendar was changed in 1752 and March became the third month instead of the first, this required long and clear instructions to all Quaker Meetings!

They regarded a lot of common etiquette as superfluity and would not bow or curtsey, doff their hats or remove them inside, or use the polite form 'you' to anyone, preferring the regular 'thee' and 'thou'. When the new convert Thomas Ellwood met his friends in Oxford, they recognized him as a Quaker because of his changed behaviour.

A knot of my old acquaintance, espying me, came to me. One of these was a scholar in his gown, another a surgeon of that city ... When they were come up to me, they all saluted me, after the usual manner, putting of their hats and bowing, and saying, 'Your humble Servant, Sir', expecting no doubt the same from me. But when they saw me stand still, not moving my cap, nor bowing my knee, in way of congee to them, they were amazed, and looked first one upon another, then upon me, then one upon another again for a while, without a word speaking. At length, the surgeon ... clapping his hand in a familiar way upon my shoulder and smiling on me said, 'What, Tom, a Quaker!' To which I readily, and cheerfully answered, 'Yes, a Quaker.' And as the words passed out of my mouth I felt joy spring into my heart, for I rejoiced that I had not been drawn out by them into a compliance with them, and that I had the strength and boldness given me to confess myself to be one of those despised people.

(*Quaker Faith and Practice*, 1995: 19.16)

Similarly, fashion was something Quakers had a particular view on. The outward, if necessary at all, was to be 'plain' and this ran through speech and dress. The uniform of the broad-rimmed hat or bonnet all in Quaker grey became a normative aspect of Quakerism only in the 18th century, but the very first Friends soon became recognizable for their plain dress.

As well as closing their shops on Wednesdays and Sundays, when Quakers came together in worship, and opening them on Christmas Day if that fell on neither a Wednesday nor a Sunday, Quaker traders bought and sold at fixed prices rather than haggle. This was an unusual practice but reflected their testimony to truth and integrity. Indeed, in the way many Quaker practices have now become generally adopted, this one gained the Quakers a reputation for honesty and led them into the nascent banking industry.

They came to opt for plain houses and 'plain' levels of consumption – a plain life. They buried their dead without the vanity of gravestones and were cautious about the frivolities of music and the theatre. When the composer Solomon Eccles joined the Friends in the 1660s, he smashed his violins – another Friend burned his ribbons. In the 19th century, this testimony to plainness would be converted to an aspiration and impellation to simplicity. Whilst testimony changed over time, it was a consequence of Quaker spiritual experience and was not optional for these early Friends. These were the saints in an apostate world, leaving their non-Quaker families, marrying only other Quakers in their own ceremonies without a minister, and in time raising their children as Quaker.

In 1650, when Fox was in Derby Jail, he was offered a captaincy in the army in exchange for his freedom but he declined, claiming he fought with spiritual weapons not outward ones. In 1660, with the restoration of the monarchy, Margaret Fell encapsulated such sentiment in a letter to the King on the peaceable nature of the Quaker people, her phrases reflected in a more public document six months later, *A Declaration from the Harmless and Innocent People of God, called Quakers*. Whilst many early Friends had served in the Parliamentary armies – Nayler had been a Quartermaster under John Lambert – the experience of convincement led them to adopt a pacifist approach and to see outward war and fighting as carnal. This aspect of testimony, typically labelled the 'peace testimony' today, became normative for Friends worldwide. Whilst some Quakers have chosen to fight in wars across the centuries, outward war as a means to resolving conflicts and creating peace has been rejected by Quakers throughout their history. In a parallel way, Quakers have built a reputation for war relief work, reconstruction, and conflict transformation.

In terms of social and political history, the situation for American Quakers differed from that in Britain. In the Puritan colony of Massachusetts, Mary Dyer and other Quakers were hanged in 1659 for their beliefs, but elsewhere, particularly in Rhode Island and Pennsylvania, Quakers were able to pioneer religious toleration. Pennsylvania was set up by William Penn, gentry convert to Quakerism in the late 1660s, whose trial with William Meade in 1670 established the right of juries to go against the advice of judges. Penn negotiated a treaty with the Native

3. Herbert Hoover (1874–1964), pictured in 1929

Americans on the land named after his father, Admiral Penn,
and attempted to establish civil government based on Quaker
principles, a 'Holy Experiment'. Quakers still had to follow the
wishes of the Crown and the Experiment was hindered from
achieving its full potential. In 1756, the Quakers left the assembly

en masse rather than vote taxes to be used for the war against the French. The difference between the American colonies and Britain is that the Quakers in the colonies decided to give up their power: in Britain, it would not be until 1870 that Quakers could be full citizens without compromise, that is, that they could join the professions or attend any university openly as a Quaker.

Quaker adaptation

By the mid-1660s, the hope that the Second Coming was unfolding was beginning to recede and was talked of less. Equally, the doctrine of perfection had to be adapted to deal with Quaker human weakness, and Friends adopted a more introspective approach. This was also a reaction to the persecution they faced under the reign of Charles II; 11,000 Quakers were imprisoned during his reign and many hundreds died.

As we see in the next chapter, Quaker theology shifted in the 18th century and was to shift again in the 19th century under the influence of the Evangelical Revival, and then again in the 20th century. Schism from the 19th century meant that by 1920, there were three clear Quaker traditions: Evangelical, Conservative, and Liberal. All maintained their testimony against worldliness, and only in the 20th century did Quakers start to celebrate Christmas and to finally drop the plain language, and the plain dress. Quakers remain 'in the world but not of it'. There have been two Quaker American Presidents, Herbert Hoover and Richard Nixon, and in Britain numerous Quaker MPs. Whilst Nixon's record in South East Asia is difficult to align with testimony against war, and his record on truth-telling at odds with Quaker testimony to integrity, his obituarists noted a particular Quaker quality to his pioneering trips to Russia and China. As the world has increasingly tolerated Quakers and has removed the obstacles to their practice, so Quakers have

4. **Richard Nixon (1913–94) visiting Pope Paul VI at the Vatican City**

tolerated the world. After 1820, they stopped seeing themselves as the true Church but rather as part of the true Church, and they worked with other Christians against slavery and for temperance. Now, in the Liberal tradition, this ecumenical spirit has given way to a broader interfaith perspective as some Friends claim non-Christian theologies or non-theist spiritualities (see Chapters 4 and 6).

The Quaker traditions

So, what of the differences between the traditions? Evangelical Friends, of holiness, fundamentalist, and modernist varieties, number 280,000 worldwide. Over half of these, and thus one-third of Friends worldwide, live in Kenya alone and there is a sizeable group in Burundi too. They are also strong in the USA, Central and Southern America, and India and Far East Asia. These groups have adopted a form of worship facilitated by a pastor and usually involving singing and, rarely, outward communion. They call themselves Friends' Churches rather than Quaker Meetings. However, along with the Conservative and Liberal Friends, they maintain a preference for peace over war and in general sit apart from the world, retaining a clear Quaker identity. Only where the church serves the community as a whole does some of the sectarian identity disappear.

The Conservative tradition can find its roots in the sectarian Quakerism that emerged in the 1660s and thereafter. These Friends worship in silence, give primary authority to the direct encounter with Christ, and conserve the Quaker traditions and testimony. They number about 1,500 worldwide and are found mainly in North America, with some adherents in Europe.

Liberal Friends have emerged out of the modernist approach favoured by some at the end of the 19th century. They place primary authority on experience and have become doctrinally permissive about matters of belief. They include, as above, non-Christian and non-theist Friends, but they have maintained the silent worship form of early Quakerism, albeit from within a different understanding. Most of the Friends in Europe and those found in Japan, Australia, New Zealand, South Africa, and Canada, as well as in parts of the USA, notably both seaboards, are Liberal. They number 55,000 worldwide.

All of these branches can trace their theological lineage back to the earliest Friends, although none of them combine all the elements of those founding days. We trace that history of evolution and revolution in the next chapter.

Chapter 2
The history of Quakerism

This chapter offers a concise overview of the history of the Quakers from the 1650s to the present day.

Early enthusiasm

The Quakers, once they had decided to set up a movement or new Church, were immensely successful at it. During the relative liberty of the 1650s, Quakers embarked on an extensive programme of mission work. Sixty to seventy pairs of itinerant preachers (like the Apostles, after Luke 10:1) travelled through England and Wales, and later Ireland, to help people turn to the new covenant with God, now freely available. In 1658, Quakers set off to convert the Pope, and Mary Fisher met with the Sultan in Constantinople. Early on, Quakers were exploring America, both for mission work and in terms of emigration. Numbers rose until about 1680, when 80,000, up to 1% of the population, were Quaker. In some places, such as the important port of Bristol, it is claimed that 10% of the population were Quaker at one point.

Quakers appear to have been very able preachers and were prolific in their tract writing. The appeal was obvious. Unlike the Calvinists, who talked of predestination, the Quakers were claiming the possibility of universal salvation. Here too was a

group without any fixed leadership or spiritual hierarchy, the
ministry open equally to men and women, with a radical spiritual
vision with radical political implications, yet retaining a clear and
strong moral line. It was an attractive mix of ideas, experience,
and possibility.

The movement also attracted a lot of hostility. The doctrine of
perfection infuriated those who placed emphasis on the sinful
nature of humanity, and the whole of Quakerism appeared
to many to be set up on a series of highly arrogant, if not
blasphemous, claims. In particular, the claim that the saints were
'as Christ', the children of God, put both George Fox and James
Nayler into jail and nearly cost Nayler his life. Enacting a sign of
Christ's Second Coming by riding a horse into Glastonbury, Wells,
and finally Bristol in 1656, surrounded by other Friends saying
'holy holy', was not unusual behaviour for these early Quakers, but
after the Bristol incident, Nayler was tried for claiming he was
Christ. The case was passed to Parliament and instead of being
hanged, he was sentenced to a public flogging, the branding of his

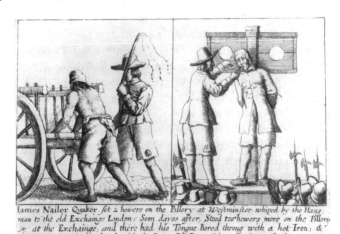

5. James Nayler's punishment, 1656

forehead with 'B' for blasphemer, and the boring of his tongue. It nearly killed him. He was then imprisoned.

Nayler was seen by many to be equal to Fox in the leadership of the movement, and for such an important Friend to be sentenced in this way was a fragile moment for the movement. Nayler had fallen out with Fox just before enacting these signs and some other Quakers criticized the enthusiasm of some of his company. There was conflict amongst Quakers in London over this, and some of Nayler's companions disrupted Quaker Meetings in the capital in a way Quakers normally did of church services. Whilst Nayler never repented to the authorities, he wrote to Friends from prison that he had allowed his 'judgement to be taken away'.

Changing doctrine

It is obviously difficult to sustain grand claims over time. What happened to the doctrine of perfection when a Quaker was found drunk in the street? If all had equal access to God's guidance, how could Quakers disagree, and how were they to know who was right when they did? If the Second Coming was unfolding and Christ was coming to all, how long was this process going to take? The doctrine of perfection was modified as early as 1653 when Quakers began to claim that different people had different 'measures' of the Inward Light. What was important was that each Friend lived up to their measure. The Quaker movement regrouped after the Nayler incident, in late 1656, partly by introducing the practice that all individual 'leadings' should be tested corporately as well. This ideal of collective reliability has been retained to this day.

The 1660s were different and difficult times for the Quaker movement. The restoration of the monarchy brought with it preventative detention, explicit legislation such as the Quaker Act of 1662 to outlaw the sect, imprisonment in large numbers, and the death of some of the leading figures. George Fox and Margaret Fell spent years in prison; Nayler was released but died in 1660. Edward Burrough died in 1662. John Perrot, one of the Friends who had undertaken the mission to the Vatican, returned to England claiming he had been given fresh revelation, that Friends should only meet when appointed to by God, and that 'hat honour' (only taking hats off to God in prayer) was to be replaced by the removal of shoes. Fox told Perrot that Quakers had received their dispensation but the disagreement led to internal schism over the legitimacy of fresh revelation and added to the challenges already placed upon Friends by the world.

The Quaker response was increasing formalization. *A Declaration from the Harmless and Innocent People of God, called Quakers*, published in 1661, formalized the testimony against outward war and fighting. In 1666, *A Testimony from the Brethren* laid out an ecclesiological discipline to 'settle' the new Church. Local meetings were grouped within 'Monthly Meetings', which met monthly to conduct their business, these grouped within 'Quarterly Meetings'; in time these all became part of the 'Yearly Meeting'. The energies of the leadership shifted from mission to internal administration. In 1671, Second Day's Morning Meeting (meeting on Monday morning) was set up as a publications committee and nothing officially Quaker was printed without their approval. 'Meeting for Sufferings' was established to petition government about the sufferings of imprisoned Friends. Separate men's and women's Business Meetings were recommended at all levels of the structure, each with their own areas of responsibility. Fox argued this was necessary for women to have their own voice, although their areas of influence were highly gendered and limited to pastoral duties such as marriage arrangements and poor relief. It seems that whilst the ideal of spiritual equality persisted, political equality did not. It was 1784 before women Friends had their own Yearly Meeting and, in Britain, only in 1909 was there a fully united men's and women's Yearly Meeting.

Quakers in the 18th century

In 1676, Robert Barclay, a second-generation gentry convert, wrote the first and one of the last systematic Quaker theologies, known popularly by its much shortened title of *The Apology*. Such systematization perhaps inevitably led to some modifications. Barclay maintained the universality of the direct encounter with God, the need to test leadings corporately, and the doctrine of perfection, but claimed it was always capable of further growth. Any mention of the Second Coming was absent from his volume and the end chapter, where it might be expected, was confined instead to advice on how to live in the world.

This kind of advice was becoming increasingly prescriptive and broad in its scope. Margaret Fell called the idea that the colour of clothing should be regulated a 'silly poor gospel', but witness moved from being consequential to convincement to a symbol of faithful waiting. For a second and third generation of Friends, brought up as Quakers by their parents, the challenge was how to be helped through life *prior* to transformation. Barclay further heightened the stakes when he wrote that, whilst everyone had their 'day of visitation' from God, if anyone should miss it, they lost their possibility of salvation. Young Quakers were brought up to wait diligently and to not let their own emotions interfere with their spiritual life: music, reading, and the theatre were considered inappropriate pursuits. Quakers could marry only other Quakers and the breaking of any of these rules could lead to 'disownment'. This became an internal Quaker version of the Christian meantime (the time of waiting before the endtimes). Quakers didn't alter the way they worshipped, as we see in the next chapter, but adopted (paradoxically) outward symbols of piety such as plain dress, plain speech, and plain living generally to separate themselves from a corrupt and corrupting world and to help them remember continually what they were about. From being co-agents with God, heralding the vanguard of the true

Church, the Quakers of the latter part of the 17th century were the gathered remnant, the true Church fearful of both God and the world. Barclay's *Apology* had the quote from the letter to Titus on its cover about being purified unto God as a 'peculiar people'. These Quakers aspired to such peculiarity.

The other paradox of this period, which we can see framing Quakerism well into the 19th century, was that, outside of the home and the Meeting House, Quakers were very involved in the nascent capitalism of the period. As well as banking, Quakers became prominent in the shoe industry and later in the iron industry (the Darbys of Coalbrookdale were Quaker) and the chocolate industry (Frys, Cadburys, and Rowntrees were all Quaker firms). Denied access as non-conformists to the English professions or British parliament, Quaker energies were directed to commerce and industry. In Darlington the football club is nicknamed 'the Quakers' as the town's fortunes were so dominated by them.

Diligent waiting rather than zealous mission work brought its own rich spirituality too. Whilst the enthusiastic and eschatological disappeared, as did some of the certainty, the claim to know God directly and to eschew any mediating text or preacher remained. To be guided was all and the primary concern was that the individual Friend was following the true guide rather than the tempter.

In the 18th century, a transatlantic Quaker community was heavily linked by kinship and commercial ties and by a common theological understanding, increasingly concerned to act with humility and diligence, an inward withdrawal in order to achieve dynamic and just action in the world. As mentioned in Chapter 1, Pennsylvania Quakers resigned almost *en masse* from their Assembly in 1756, thus ending the 'Holy Experiment', as part of wider reformation within the movement. Meetings were concerned to preserve and present purity, and the 'travelling

6. 'William Penn's treaty with the Indians', Pennsylvania, 1681

ministry' of Friends given a certificate of release was usually
directed at those who were already Quakers rather than potential
converts.

In the journal of the New Jersey Friend, John Woolman
(1720–72), we find the unfolding spiritual journey of someone
open to being led by God, as well as the clarity of his 'concerns'
for war-tax resistance, Native American rights, the plight of
the poor, and that American Friends join him in his stance
against slave-holding. He sold the family business and wore only
undyed clothing, as dyes were produced from work done by slaves.
When he felt he had been unfaithful, he was laid low in bed until
he felt forgiven and restored. Everything was to be led by God.
Other examples of this approach can be found in deliberations
over marriage. Catherine Phillips waited 23 years before being
clear that she had found the right partner. Joseph Conran felt
a 'draft of love more than natural' (that is, supernatural and

PLATE 4.—ELIZABETH FRY IN NEWGATE.

7. Elizabeth Fry (1780–1845) speaking to inmates of Newgate Prison

therefore to be trusted) when he first saw Louisa Strongman (Damiano, 1988, p. 184). He felt sure she was to be his wife: two years later, he told her, and six years later, they were married. Quakers were equally concerned about the 'what' as well as the 'when'.

Norwich Friend Elizabeth Gurney (later Fry) (1780–1845) wore scarlet laces in purple boots under her Quaker grey but was persuaded to a more diligent life by American travelling minister William Savery. Moving to London with her husband, she became involved with women prisoners awaiting transportation at Newgate jail. She helped thousands prepare for their journeys, providing them with quilting kits so they would have produce to sell when they reached Australia. Her work was part of the ongoing Quaker concern for penal reform.

Pioneers like Woolman and Fry were not always celebrated in their own lifetimes. Woolman's witness was not always affirmed by the groups he visited, and Fry was disciplined when some of her children married non-Quakers. Later Quakerism rehabilitated the reputation of these great reformers.

Quakers in the 19th century

The 19th century saw the end of Quakerism as a single community and, with it, the end of the claim that Quakerism represented the true Church. These two factors are related and link to the influence of the Evangelical Revival on Quakerism, firstly in the USA, then in Britain. This brought about internal theological dispute but also encouraged Quakers to see themselves not as the true Church but as *part* of the true Church, that is, as part of a wider Christianity.

The initial faultline that developed within the transatlantic community can be identified in a number of ways. Theologically, it ran between those influenced by the Evangelical Revival, who wished Quakerism to become more evangelical with greater authority placed on scripture, and those who took the interiority of Quaker spirituality to such an extreme degree as to resist anything outward, even scriptural teachings. Both innovative, these groups become known in America as the Orthodox and the Hicksites (after Elias Hicks) respectively, and the division between them as the Great Separation. In direct contrast to the most extreme of the Hicksites, some of whom were deist, the Orthodox emphasized the role of scripture to a greater degree, even to the point of equality to, or authority over, the Inward Light, of which they were wary. One English group of Quaker Evangelicals, called the Beaconites, believed the Inward Light to be delusional.

Sociologically, the Orthodox were generally the urban elite of Quaker Meetings and often those acting as Elders within the Meetings. The Hicksites were often more rural, more concerned with discipline rather than doctrine. They included some concerned with the radical politics of the French Revolution and those in touch with other prophetic movements. Both sides were innovative of the tradition in their own ways, and both sides included those who emphasized diligence and peculiarity. As is typical of schism, many on either side were unaware of the main issues and found themselves labelled by family ties or, ultimately, because they attended one Meeting or another.

In Britain, Evangelicals gained influence from the beginning of the 19th century and were more publicly dominant by the 1820s. The 300 or so Beaconites only broke away in the 1830s because of their extreme position on the Inward Light, most British Friends by this stage balancing the authority of scripture and direct revelation. They were drawn together by kinship, small numbers (shrinking since 1680 and further depleted by mass disownments, for example, for 'marrying out'), geography, and continuing restrictions placed on their activity by the state.

In America, the two groups reached a point in 1827 when division seemed inevitable and even desirable as both sides wished to purify and 'restore' Quakerism. After the Philadelphia Yearly Meeting that year, two Yearly Meetings existed there, one Orthodox, one Hicksite. Other American Yearly Meetings also divided in the years that followed.

Each side struggled to maintain control of the Meeting House and the minute book, symbols of the inheritance both regarded themselves to be part of. Each side disowned the other *en masse*. The Orthodox disowned the Hicksites for their wayward theology; the Hicksites disowned the Orthodox for their poor discipline. Where one group lost the Meeting House, they built another, sometimes just across the street.

In the 1840s and 1850s, the Orthodox Yearly Meetings underwent further schism over the continually vexed question of the role of the Inward Light. Quaker Joseph John Gurney (Elizabeth Fry's brother), highly influential in Britain, embarked in 1837 on a three-year speaking tour of the States, to find his views opposed by John Wilbur of Rhode Island. Gurney claimed the role of the Inward Light was to help Friends read scripture correctly in the spirit in which it had been given. Wilbur thought Gurney too worldly and this view of the Inward Light too innovative. Wilbur, rather, saw himself as a traditional Friend, balancing the authority given revelation with scripture. New England Yearly Meeting, who were persuaded by Gurney, disowned Wilbur and most of his Meeting in 1843, and this ultimately led to two New England Yearly Meetings in 1844. Yearly Meetings traditionally sent their greetings and news to each other each year. Schism spread because other Yearly Meetings needed to decide which Yearly Meeting's epistle to accept. Philadelphia circumvented the problem by refusing to engage in any epistolary correspondence. When the Ohio Orthodox Yearly Meeting split in 1854, it meant that there were then three Ohio Yearly Meetings – Hicksite, Gurneyite, and Wilburite.

To the outsider, all three groupings may have been indistinguishable. All worshipped in silence in Meeting Houses, all maintained a distinct way of conducting church business, all dressed and spoke in the peculiar Quaker fashion, all maintained their witness against war and against slave-holding. Thousands of slaves were helped escape through the 'underground railroad' run by Quakers, where homes would operate as safe stations for the 'locomotive'. More visible perhaps than the theological divisions which underlay the schisms were the differing views on a) how far Quakers should join with non-Quakers in their witness work, and b) whether this should involve breaking the law. These issues were a cause of tension in all three groups. In 1842, Indiana Yearly Meeting (Gurneyite) divided over the commitment of some Friends there against slavery even if it involved law-breaking. The schism lasted a decade.

Based on doctrinal unity, matters of belief and interpretation were more likely to cause division in the Gurneyite branch, and in the late 1860s the influence of Camp Revival Meetings created two tendencies within the Gurneyite group: Renewal/modernist and Revival/holiness.

Renewal Quakerism was in some ways a natural development of Gurneyite 'world-accepting' Quakerism. It wanted to move on from the peculiarities and have a modern Quakerism of its time, 'renewed', and work with other Christians in bringing about the Kingdom. Theologically, they were post-millennial, that is, they believed humanity would prepare the way for the rule of the saints and the subsequent Second Coming of Christ.

Revival Quakerism was equally explicitly meantime in its theology but pre-millennial: Christ would initiate the rule of the saints and human endeavour was limited in efficacy. These Quakers were wary of the world and its ways and, whilst influenced by the interdenominational holiness movement, more guarded about wider alliances. Central to them was the transformative experiences of conversion, a first blessing, and of the second blessing, sanctification. Unlike early Friends, this group separated the two experiences and the leading holiness Friend David Updegraff experienced sanctification, when 'every vile affection was nailed to the cross' (Hamm, 1988, p. 78), nine years after his conversion experience.

Revival Friends rejected the peculiarities as the world's people, such as Hicksites, were maintaining their use. After 1867, Revival Meetings became regular additions to silent worship. They involved preaching, spontaneous experience, emotional expression, and music, and brought thousands of converts into Quakerism. The Indiana Gurneyite Yearly Meeting grew by 50% in a nine-year period.

These converts needed induction into the Quaker faith, and ministry to nurture their spiritual journeys. Instead, they often found silent meetings very different from the Revival meetings that had attracted them to the sect. General Meetings were established to help with faith transmission, but these developed into devotional meetings. Rather than separate different kinds of worshippers, pastoral committees were set up to help the teaching ministry, but these quickly led to the 'release' (payment) of pastors. The first Quaker pastor began work in 1875, and by 1900 most American Gurneyite Yearly Meetings had accepted this innovation.

This was not without controversy, of course, and further schism took place in some Yearly Meetings. Those that left found they worked most easily with Wilburite Friends, and together they formed the Conservative tradition.

At the same time, those who were left were faced by another challenge, that of the desire on the part of some Friends to undergo water baptism. The outward sacraments were one of the few differences between Revival Friends and other Christians, and David Updegraff led 'the water party' in seeking toleration for water baptism of ministers. Only in his native Ohio did he find widespread support, and in 1878 the Richmond Declaration of Faith, drawn up at a meeting of all Gurneyite Yearly Meetings including Britain, clearly stated the traditional Quaker position in favour of inward baptism rather than outward. This Declaration not only settled this dispute for Gurneyite Friends but became a measure of orthodoxy within that tradition. It was adopted by most of the Yearly Meetings who gathered to discuss it and remains at the front of the Books of Discipline of many of these bodies to this day.

The division over water baptism weakened Revival Quakerism, as did an internal divide over speaking in tongues following the

8. Lucretia Mott (1793–1880)

Pentecostal revival of 1905. Renewal/modernist Friends became more dominant after this point, helped by the writing and campaigning of Rufus Jones (1867–1948). The American Yearly Meetings which met at Richmond in 1878 went on to meet every five years and set up Five Years Meeting (FYM) in 1902, and this then became Friends United Meeting (FUM), a group that today encompasses both modernist and fundamentalist views.

Ohio never joined Five Years Meeting and formed an alliance with Yearly Meetings that left FYM and FUM through the 20th century. Today they form Evangelical Friends International (EFI).

The Hicksites did not suffer doctrinal division but did suffer some small-scale schism over structure and discipline. Friends who labelled themselves 'Progressives' broke away, seeking greater independence, in effect congregationalism, and to pursue a more radical political agenda over slave-holding and women's rights. Others pursued this agenda within the Hicksite fold. Lucretia Mott (1793–1880), for example, worked tirelessly for the abolition of slavery, joining with those outside her own Hicksite tradition to do so. She co-founded the Philadelphia Female Anti-Slavery Society, which was interracial and interdenominational. In 1840, she travelled to London to attend the World Anti-Slavery Convention. She was denied a seat as she was a woman and this led her, with other women (mostly Quaker), to organize the Seneca Falls Convention for women's rights of 1848. Mott was also an advocate of peaceful non-resistance, Native American rights, temperance and prison reform. Mott was one of many Hicksites who began to call for a more rational approach to the reading of scripture and the use of scholarship to better understand its provenance. This modernist approach was normative within the Hicksite branch by the 1870s, and in the 20th century they are best described as Liberal Yearly Meetings. Like the Gurneyite Friends, but for different reasons to do with a more relaxed attitude to the world, these Friends also dropped most of the peculiarities. In America, these Yearly

Meetings formed an umbrella association called Friends' General Conference.

Quakers in the 20th century

In Britain, the Evangelicals also reformed the peculiarities. Their concern was the impediment it gave to conversion, especially as membership had reached a low of about 14,000 in the late 1850s, as well as the fact that other Christians, who dressed or spoke 'normally' seemed none for the worse for it. Gravestones were allowed after 1850, the rule about marrying out was modified in 1860 (a Friend could marry a non-Friend but only in a Meeting House), and in 1861 plain dress and speech became optional. In time, however, this greater freedom to engage with the world led British Evangelicals to their own demise. Younger Friends were attracted by biblical scholarship, and higher criticism, and in a very rapid shift, Gurneyite Quakerism in Britain was replaced by a Liberal/modernist approach. The Manchester Conference of 1895 saw both Evangelical and Liberal views expressed, but following the conference the momentum of the Liberal revisioning of Quakerism grew. John Wilhelm Rowntree was the leading architect of Liberal Quakerism in Britain. In 1897, he met with Rufus Jones whilst on holiday and the two became great friends and allies. Both organized summer schools and planned a new history of Quakerism which, they envisaged, would reinvigorate the movement and bring it back to its mystical roots. Education was key to the modernist approach. Rowntree died in 1905, but the shift in Britain was secure by then and underpins the kind of Quakerism we find there today.

Throughout the theological shifts of the late 19th century, mission work became increasingly important for all Gurneyite Yearly Meetings. In Britain, the adult school movement began in the late 1840s and the home mission movement soon after. Popular devotional meetings were organized to sit alongside the literacy work of the adult schools. After 1860, British and American

9. Ramallah Quaker Mission School, photographed in 1937

Friends looked to overseas mission work as well, and Friends went to India and China. In 1902, three American Friends landed in Mombassa and set up a mission on the other side of Kenya. By 1914, there were only 50 converts, but today over one-third of the world's Quakers can be found in Kenya. Mission to South America in the 1920s and after has also led to significant numbers of Friends there, especially in Bolivia and Peru (see Chapter 7).

For the modernist Yearly Meetings, mission work became more focused on social justice in the 20th century. After 1870, Friends in Britain enjoyed full citizenship and for 40 years enjoyed this sense of respectability and purpose. A number followed John Bright's example and became MPs, and it seemed the more the state tolerated Quakerism, the more Quakers accepted the state. The introduction of conscription in 1916 changed this relationship, and Friends again found themselves protesting and law-breaking. The Friends Ambulance Unit offered alternative service, but 145 British Quakers refused any kind of alternative service and were imprisoned.

In America, Rufus Jones, having created a modernist agenda for FYM, worked with (even!) Hicksites on social justice and peace issues. In 1917, the American Friends Service Committee was set up, funded by a number of different Yearly Meetings, to carry out peace work and feeding programmes during and in the aftermath of World War I. Thousands were helped in Poland, Russia, and Austria in particular. In the 1930s, the same organization helped provide work and food for starving miners in the Appalachian Mountains, whilst in Britain the Quakers organized projects for the miners of Bryn Mawr and Maes-y-Haf. Similarly, Friends helped with food supplies and refugees in the Spanish Civil War. After World War II, Quakers worked extensively in Germany helping with reconstruction and with food supplies. The work of the Quakers following both world wars was acknowledged in 1947 when the Nobel Peace Prize was jointly awarded to British and American Friends.

Peace and social justice work paved the way for Friends across the different branches of Quakerism to begin to talk to each other again, and in 1945 the Wilburite and Gurneyite Yearly Meetings in New England became one again. In 1955, three Canadian Yearly Meetings reunited, as did two each in New York and Philadelphia, and Baltimore consolidated in 1967.

The 20th century for Quakerism can be characterized in terms of mission and the growth of modernism. Some Evangelical Friends and Liberal Quakers are very different from each other, but the commonalities listed at the top of the previous chapter remain: the sense of direct encounter with God; reliance on God's guidance in life and in church business; the spiritual equality of all; the testimony to peace and social justice. We look at the nature of Quaker worship in more depth next.

Chapter 3
Worship

As mentioned above, the initial understanding of Quaker worship was framed by a keen sense of the unfolding and inward Second Coming of Christ. However, in its basic form, it has endured beyond that interpretation and remains a central distinction of Quakers worldwide, as well as one of their binding forces.

The basis of Quaker worship

The experience of George Fox in 1647 that 'there was one, even Christ Jesus, that can speak to thy condition' established the primacy of direct revelation and the interiority of authentic spirituality. Outward forms of religion, outward liturgical forms and practices, were all seen to belong to an age that had now passed. Through the Quakers, God was establishing a new covenant with humanity, and the long-awaited Second Coming of Christ was unfolding inwardly, after Jeremiah 31: 31–34. Critically, this was not to be confined to a select group but was an experience that was universally available; everyone could be part of the elect.

Borrowing from the Seekers' use of silent worship and affirming its use by reference to Revelation 8:1 (and the half-hour of silence in Heaven after the breaking of the seventh seal), Quakers adopted a 'liturgy of silence' in which absence gave way to a sense of the presence. References to Zephaniah and Habbakuk, amongst others, affirmed the value of silence. Through silence, Quakers claimed, God could be best encountered and heard. This was the medium of approach to God, and the medium for experience of God. This experience gave authority for belief and silence would also be used as the basis for making business decisions, as all was to be put before God. In this way, the use of silence ran throughout the devotional and practical aspects of church life. We return to this in Chapter 5.

> Though it was silent from words, yet the word of the Lord God was among us; it was as a hammer and a fire; it was sharper than any two-edged sword; it pierced through our inward parts; it melted and brought us into tears that there was scarcely a dry eye among us. The Lord's blessed power overshadowed our meeting, and I could have said that God alone was master of that assembly.
>
> (Kirk, 1978, p. 91)

It was not that these Quakers eschewed the sacraments, rather they encompassed them in a new way within their silent and inward approach to God. As mentioned in Chapter 1, Revelation 3:20 talks of the inward supper, and instead of the focus for the Lord's supper being on breaking the bread until the Lord comes again, as in 1 Cor 11:26, Fox talked of the marriage supper of the Lamb. Quakers believed in baptism by the Spirit and could find plenty of scriptural affirmation for that (for example, Mark 1:8).

For those who had experienced the transformation of convincement, the whole of life had a sacramental quality to it, but the early Quakers also emphasized the need and benefit of worshipping corporately. After the James Nayler incident (related in Chapter 2), this collective approach was also seen as a more reliable mode of discerning God's guidance. Worshipping together increased both the effect and efficacy of the liturgical act.

The Lord of heaven and earth we found to be near at hand, and, as we waited upon him in pure silence, our mind out of all things, His heavenly presence appeared in our assemblies, when there was no language, tongue nor speech from any creature. The kingdom of heaven did gather us and catch us all, as in a net, and His heavenly power at one time drew many hundreds to land. We came to know a place to stand in and what to wait in; and the Lord appeared daily to us, to our astonishment, amazement, and great admiration, insomuch that we often said one unto another, with great joy of heart: 'What, is the kingdom of God come to be with men? And will he take up His tabernacle among the sons of men, as He did of old? And what? Shall we, that were reckoned as the outcasts of Israel, have this honour of glory communicated amongst others, as amongst men?' And from that day forward, our hearts were knit unto the Lord and one another in true and fervent love, in the covenant of Life with God; and that was a strong bond upon our spirits, which united us one to another.

(*Quaker Faith and Practice*, 1995: 19.08)

Whilst silence was valued above outward speech, 'vocal ministry' (that is, any contribution given to the speaker from God) was an accepted part of Quaker worship. Anyone in worship might potentially be given something to share – all were spiritually equal and all were part of the priesthood – and Meetings, as worship was called, whilst based in silence, could be filled with preaching; Fox could easily preach for over an hour. Worship itself was typically three hours long in the 17th century, but some Meetings were recorded as being of nine hours' duration.

As mentioned at the start of the book, 'Quaker' was originally a pejorative term applied by Justice Bennett when Fox was on trial in Derby in 1650, and referred to the way the early Friends shook and trembled during worship. The body became the site, the location, of spiritual experience and revelation: Christ dwelled within. There was often a physical aspect to worship, particularly for women Friends, and anti-Quaker tracts particularly played upon Quaker women's expression, sexualizing it or casting it as dangerous to the onlooker. For Friends, physical expression was another version of the signs they felt impelled by God to act out, to help bring the apostate into the true Church.

Quaker worship in the 18th century

By the 1670s, Quakers were not proclaiming the unfolding Second Coming as they had before. They still felt drawn into a spiritual intimacy with God, and acting as co-agents with God in and against 'the world', but they no longer framed their understanding of worship in eschatological terms. Barclay, in omitting references to the Second Coming from *The Apology*, and Quaker theologians after him, shifted the terms of the debate over communion. They did not follow Fox in talking of the marriage supper of the Lamb, but argued over the meaning of the 1 Cor 11:26 verse and how far it was an instruction to institute a rite.

Quakerism could have changed the way it worshipped. Moving into a meantime perspective from an endtime one could have allowed Friends to adopt all the well-tried meantime practices of other Christians, to help its community wait faithfully. They could have appointed particular ministers, followed the Christian calendar, and practised a more outward liturgy. In one way they did. From the 18th century, those with the 'gift of ministry' were recorded by their Monthly Meetings. Late 17th- and 18th-century Meeting Houses were built with a two-tier facing bench to seat the Elders and above them these Ministers. However, worship remained rooted in silence, the means to the direct experience of God that lay at the basis of Quakerism; even if it was interpreted slightly differently now, revelation was still the primary aspect of Quaker spirituality.

As the claims to the unfolding Second Coming fell away, so did the more physical aspects of worship. The second and third generations played down the ecstatic nature of the first, and even

10. Friends Meeting House, Quaker Street Village, New York, built in 1807

amended some of the language used by George Fox to describe the relationship between the saints and Christ. The enactment of signs fell away and could even be a matter for internal discipline.

In the 18th century, the diligence at the heart of Quietism became the main focus of worship. Quakers felt they needed to be open and aware of God but wary and guarded in terms of the world, including their own emotions, imaginations, and human 'willings and runnings'. Sarah Lynes Grubb wrote in 1780:

> I am often afraid lest by indulging my own ideals of what is good, and not labouring after a total resignation of mind ... I should frustrate the divine intention, which may be to humble and reduce self more than flesh and blood would point out.
>
> (Jones, 1921, p. 68)

Silence easily accommodated this spiritual stance – diligence, after all, had always been a part of Quakerism, simply coupled

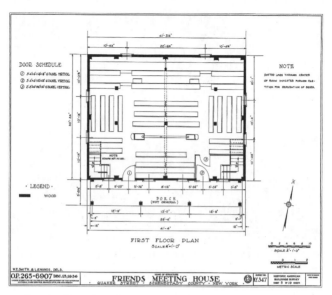

DOOR SCHEDULE

NOTE

DOTTED LINES THROUGH CENTER
OF ROOM INDICATES FORMER PAR-
TITION FOR SEPARATION OF SEXES.

· LEGEND ·

WOOD

PORCH
(NOT ORIGINAL)

FIRST FLOOR PLAN
SCALE ¼"=1'-0"

SCALE ¼"=1'-0"

METRIC SCALE

W.E.SMITH & L.G.WANDS, DEL.S.

O.P.265-6907 DEC.15,1936

FRIENDS MEETING HOUSE
QUAKER STREET · SCHENECTADY COUNTY · NEW YORK

NY.347

11. Interior floor plan, showing the position of the benches and centre partition

with less caution and anxiety – but Meetings became shorter and less vibrant. In some of them, monitors were appointed to awaken the sleeping. Anxieties over ministering faithfully could lead to meeting after meeting being wholly silent, but could equally lead a Quaker to be miserable should they have been silent when they should have spoken. In this case, John Stubbs did not minister when he had been prompted but then, feeling his lack of obedience, ministered later without divine prompting:

> I never fell into more disobedience than last meeting at thy house, and was warned of it before, for, when the spring and well was set open, but then I did not speak, but in the dread I spoke, but the life was shut up, and I felt it to my condemnation.

(Bauman, 1983, p. 131)

Anxiety of course also acted as a form of control. The free ministry is very open to abuse, intentional and otherwise, hence the use of Elders to nurture and discipline worship. In the 18th century, Quakers began to minister in a nasal or sing-song tone to differentiate their human voice from what God was giving them to say. Everything about Quaker worship was 'unnatural' or unworldly, and this sharp distinction between the silence of worship and the talk of the world helped Quakers remember what they were about.

Thus, whilst they did not adopt meantime liturgical forms, they adopted a form of liturgy that helped them remain faithful in the meantime. Speaking and dressing differently also helped them retain a clear dualism between themselves as the gathered remnant and the world. In this way, they had their own outward forms to complement the distinctive and unchanged mode of worship.

Diversity in Quaker worship

Quaker worship has become shorter by about half an hour a century, and the focus of the vocal ministry changed in line with the changing focus of the group. However, the 19th century brought the greatest innovation as the idea of the Inward Light became questioned by those influenced by the Evangelical Revival. Some considered it a delusion or subject to the imagination, a critique which horrified the more ardent Quietists who were equally wary of 'imagination'.

Unlike Hicksite and Wilburite Quakerism, Gurneyite Friends moved from a strict reliance on direct guidance from God through the Inward Light of Christ to a place where scriptural authority became primary. The Inward Light, for example for Joseph John Gurney, helped Quakers read scripture in the right way but had no independent authority and was certainly not of higher

43

authority than scripture. Gurney never questioned the silent form of worship (and Evangelicals were never totally without opposition within British Quakerism), although that was a logical next step for some, such as the Beaconites. When the Manchester Beaconites split away in 1836, they built a chapel and instituted worship with hymns and preaching akin to other Protestant denominations.

In the United States, such innovation was easier to accommodate without schism. Through the 1860s and 1870s, as mentioned in the previous chapter, interdenominational holiness Meetings became highly influential amongst some Gurneyite Friends and they started to model devotional 'General Meetings' on them. These would include music, altar calls, mourners' benches, handkerchief salutes to those who have passed on before, highly expressive preaching and vocal testimony, and they resembled the holiness meetings of other Churches far more than anything ever seen before in Quakerism.

Late in the summer of 1875 a Methodist minister decided to indulge his professional curiosity by attending the annual gathering of Indiana Yearly Meeting Friends in Richmond. Unlike his military brother fourteen years before, the Methodist minister felt completely at home. The devotional meeting opened with the singing of a familiar hymn. Then the presiding preacher called for testimonies. Within ninety minutes nearly 300 people had spoken. Then an altar call was issued, and soon seekers after conversion and sanctification crowded around several mourners' benches. To the Methodist visitor, it all had a familiar feeling. 'It resembled one of our best *love feasts* at a *National Camp Meeting* [more] than anything else to which I could liken it,' he told the leading interdenominational holiness journal. The scenes in Richmond were not unusual for Gurneyite Friends in 1875. They had set an unprecedented course.

(Hamm, 1988, p. 74)

At the same time, holiness Friends could find ample precedent for this style of worship in the expressive evangelism of the first Friends.

These holiness Friends were still concerned about the meantime, expecting the endtime at some point but not experiencing its unfolding in the present. In this regard, they were simply adopting an alternative meantime liturgical form, a different way of waiting faithfully. Critically, the direct experience of God still lay the heart of the holiness devotional meeting. Indeed, it was far more evident to them there than in some of the totally silent regular Quaker Meetings. Conversion and sanctification, whilst separated by these Quakers, were distinct moments of transformation, experienced by thousands. Quaker faith was outwardly vibrant and embodied once again. In time, the pull came to substitute elements of these additional devotional meetings for the regular silent worship. The catalyst for such a radical innovation of form was the desire to enhance the teaching ministry, given the thousands of newcomers attending Quaker Meetings. Pastoral committees were established, but these were soon converted into single person pastorates. As mentioned in Chapter 2, the first Quaker pastor was released in 1875 and most Gurneyite Yearly Meetings in the USA had pastors by 1900.

Pastors were not priests; everyone was still spiritually equal. Rather, a pastor was someone serving the Meeting to help enhance and lead worship. Very quickly, those Meetings with pastors changed from the 'unprogrammed' silent format to what can be called 'programmed' worship. In other words, there are a number of different elements to worship, such as singing and preaching, praise, and prayer, which are pre-programmed before the event, as opposed to the single activity of silent waiting. Both are programmed in one way but the pastor or pastoral team needs to make a decision about content and order. Having said this, most Quaker pastors today

12. The congregation of the Friends' Church, Dead Ox Flat, Oregon, 1939

claim to exercise 'discernment' about this, and are prepared to change the order should they feel God guiding them to, even mid-worship.

New Meeting Houses in the pastoral tradition started to look different from the more traditional ones. They required more of an explicit 'front', perhaps a pulpit, or a space for a choir, an organ. They needed to be bigger. And, drawn into this reinvention of Quakerism by an increasing sense of allegiance to wider Christianity, Meeting Houses began to look more like, and to be called, churches, in some cases with bell towers, if not steeples.

Pastoral Quakerism today

Pastoral Quakerism extended beyond holiness Quakerism and today covers a wide theological spectrum, including modernist, holiness, and fundamentalist perspectives. Today, pastoral

Quakerism extends across the whole of the USA, Central and South America, East Africa, and parts of Asia. Mission work continues to take this tradition to new locations. Some of these Friends' Churches follow the Christian calendar and a few have initiated a monthly or twice annual outward communion. From the 1880s, some have tolerated or offered water baptism.

Mostly Friends' churches, especially in the USA, are still distinctively Quaker. Silence still lies at the heart of the programming, and all the other elements of worship can be seen to prepare the worshipper for that period of inward communion. It may be short, sometimes as little as ten minutes, but it remains central. Where the holiness tradition has been particularly influential, the silence may be filled with testimony and prayer and the sense of inward communion lost or misunderstood, but in many Friends' Churches the intention of the 'open worship' is explicit. In this, in spite of the adoption of other more mainstream meantime practices, these churches are still distinctively Quaker.

At one Friends' Church, 'Meeting for Worship' lasts 75 minutes and typically comprises: a musical 'prelude'; opening words of welcome from one of the pastors; a hymn; welcomes, announcements, and prayers for those in need, including a prayer for the person giving 'the message' (that they may be given the words 'you want us to hear'); the narrative – a reading or, for example, a dramatic interpretation of a scriptural passage; music to accompany the offertory; 'choruses' (less formal than the hymn with repeated sections as led by the 'worship leader'); the message, lasting around 15 minutes; up to 15 minutes of 'open worship' ('Communion after the Manner of Friends'); prior to closing music and closing words from one of the pastors. The pattern varies week to week. This church has its own choir and its own handbell group. Visiting speakers may give the message, or there may be a particular focus, for example at Pentecost or Christmas.

Some Meetings are semi-programmed and may have up to an hour of programming and an hour of silent worship.

'Unprogrammed' Quakers and worship

The Conservatives, some of whom originated in schisms over the introduction of pastors (see Chapter 2), and Liberal Friends continue without pastors and programming. A Conservative Quaker introductory leaflet reads:

> We gather in expectant silence to wait upon the Lord. When we gather in His name, Christ Jesus is truly here with us. Therefore we do not seek to worship, pray or sing in our own wisdom or strength, but to hear what the True Shepherd would have us do. The hour of worship is His, to program as He sees fit: our task is to respond with the worship, prayer, ministry, or song that He gives us.

> ('Welcome to Our Meeting',
> Ohio Yearly Meeting (Conservative), n.d.)

Seats are arranged in a circle or square, usually in an unadorned room. Participants come into the room silently and sit where they wish. Worship usually lasts an hour. Participants talk of 'centring down' into the silence. The whole time may be silent or it may be that some present share 'vocal ministry' with the rest of the group. Typically, there are three or four ministries in the hour, each lasting three or four minutes. The end of worship is signalled by the shaking of hands, initiated by one of two 'Elders', the only pre-arranged outward gesture of the whole rite. Some Meetings that are particularly deep are referred to as 'covered' or 'gathered'. It remains a stark contrast to the way most other Christians worship, and the very layout of the room reflects the foundational insight of the Quaker group, that all can equally have direct experience of God.

Vocal ministry in unprogrammed worship

The experience underpinning unprogrammed and open worship is very different from that envisaged in the 1650s. Only a few Friends today seem to undergo the painful and totally life-changing transformation of the first Quaker leaders. As such, the experience underpinning vocal ministry has changed. In the 19th and 20th centuries, the nasal tone of the Quietists was replaced by Quakers no longer concerned to speak in their voice. Human agency became elevated, but with it, the dangers of mistaking where ministry comes from. A flow chart is given out in one Friends' Church to help the Friends there discern whether what they have to say is vocal ministry or just a good idea. It asks if the message is from God or the self, if the message is for the individual or the group, whether the message need be shared outwardly, and whether the God-given message need be shared outwardly with the group *now*. Answering 'yes' to all these is seen to validate the prompting to speak. Whilst the chart is given out to help explain the process to newcomers, many Quakers who have ministered say they found themselves on their feet and cannot remember what they said.

Ministry is not 'normal' speech. As expected in a group with so unbounded a theory of worship and ministry, there are codes and rules to help protect the experience of worship. Sociologically, there are seven aspects to typical ministry: i) length; ii) style; iii) frequency; iv) timing; v) content; vi) theming; vii) construction. In a survey of 14 Meetings, the length of ministry ranged between 7 and 20 minutes for the whole Meeting. Individual ministries ranged between 20 seconds and just over 10 minutes; 70% of the spoken contributions were less than 3 minutes in duration. Ministries which are of a length greater than 10 to 15 minutes may be publicly interrupted by an Elder trying to restore order. This is not an easy task, as ministry is notionally from God and Elders have to weigh that 'divine potential' against the need to nurture worship for all. (Similarly, if Elders go to close the Meeting and someone rises to minister, the ministry has higher authority.)

It was mentioned above that Friends used to minister in a nasal tone to differentiate between their own words and those of God. Present-day Friends do not mask their own voices in the same way but do subdue their voices. Displays of emotion are rare.

The advice is to minister no more than once in Meeting for Worship. In a disrupted Meeting containing 11 ministries, four from one person, it was the multiple nature of the contributions, rather than their length or style, which allowed an Elder to intervene. Timing is important too.

> Wait to be sure of the right moment for giving the message ...
> Beware of making additions towards the end of a meeting when it
> was well left before.
>
> (*Quaker Faith and Practice*, 1995: 2.55)

There are 'non-mentionables', such as insults, contributions which require an answer (such as the making of arrangements), and items which have no relevance or significance to the group. Ministry needs to fit in with the values and sensibilities of the Meeting. The normal pattern is for ministry to add to the theme of the opening contribution. The repetition of key phrases and back and forward references to other ministries and even other Meetings are normal.

There is also a particular format of ministry which is common. It begins with a story or anecdote, then connects this with a key theological or political insight. This is an acknowledged pattern and some Quakers claim an anecdotal opening helps them adjust to sound coming out of silence in time to fully hear the more important part of the message.

Some of these patterns are to do with the Meeting as a social event, others to do with protecting it from worldly custom. As mentioned above, a 'free ministry' is potentially risky, as Meetings could easily be taken over or disrupted. What is perhaps surprising is how rare that is and how outwardly uniform they are.

In terms of the inward, studies show that Friends are engaged in many different kinds of activity, often in parallel or tandem in any one Meeting. They may be praying or praising or seeking communion or guidance, thinking, or sleeping. Two-thirds of Liberal Friends in one study said that 'thinking' best described what they were doing in Meeting. In the early 20th century, one Friend was interrupted by an Elder for beginning a ministry with 'I was thinking', as thought was not considered appropriate activity. Whilst the form has altered little since the earlier days,

13. Interior, Quaker Meeting House, Easton, MD. The partitions used to divide men's and women's Business Meetings in the past are clearly visible

the understanding of what is happening in worship and the content of the silence has changed dramatically.

New Quakers 'learn' the silence and the rules about ministry by sitting and watching. Whilst one or two mention anxiety on first attending in case they were meant to speak next, the ideal is that the total newcomer is told about the overall pattern of worship and finds it helpful. There is never any pressure to minister. Few minister in the first three months of attending, and most of those who do at all find it was one to three years after first attending before they spoke in Meeting.

Quaker Meetings for business

Business Meetings follow a similar pattern in all the traditions and utilize silence as a way to approach the discernment of God's will. The Meeting appoints 'Clerks' to help introduce the business to the Meeting and to record its decisions in minutes. Clerks 'serve' the Meeting and their responsibilities are very explicit. The role is rotated every few years through the members of the Meeting. They do not lead the group and neither should they express a view on 'the matter before the Meeting'. They are there to help the Meeting remember its own discipline, that it is part of worship to try to 'discern' God's will. In small groups especially, it can be easy for a Meeting to lapse into discussion or conversation rather than discernment. Standing to speak is one of the ways Friends remember the discipline, addressing comments to 'the table' (the Clerk or Clerks), in a large Meeting speaking only once on any one matter, or in a very large Meeting waiting for the Clerk to discern who to call to speak. The Clerk also discerns when to attempt to write a minute to reflect the 'sense of the Meeting'. This can only be done once there is a clear agreement on what to do. The Clerk or 'Recording Clerk' drafts a minute and then, or at a later time, reads it to the Meeting. Subsequent contributions are on the wording of the minute only, until it can be accepted by the Meeting. Once the minute is accepted, the Meeting moves on to the next item on the agenda. No votes are taken. One of the signs Quakers use to be more sure they are in line with God's will is the sense of unity they feel. If they are not largely in unity, the discernment needs to continue. If unity cannot be found, the matter is postponed. It can be a slow process and potentially a conservative one, relying on all to agree. At the same time, the whole process is considered one of worship and the unexpected and radical can suddenly find great unity. Participants are asked to be open to follow God's guidance and not come to a Meeting with mind made up but with 'heart and mind prepared'.

> In our meetings for worship we seek through the stillness to know God's will for ourselves and for the gathered group. Our meetings for church affairs, in which we conduct our business, are also meetings for worship based on silence, and they carry the same expectation that God's guidance can be discerned if we are truly listening together and to each other, and are not blinkered by preconceived opinions. It is this belief that God's will can be recognised through the discipline of silent waiting which distinguishes our decision-making process from the secular idea of consensus. We have a common purpose in seeking God's will through waiting and listening, believing that every activity of life should be subject to divine guidance.

> (*Quaker Faith and Practice*, 1995: 3.02)

Those who are not there need to trust the process was 'truly led'.

This same process is used for all Quaker committees and Business Meetings in all the traditions. It is used, for example, by a 'Nominations Committee' to select a name to put to the Meeting to become the next 'Clerk' or 'Overseer'. It is used by a Meeting to discuss applications for formal membership. It is used to discuss action required in an emergency. There is a Quaker postcard which reads: 'I am a Quaker: in case of emergency, please be silent.' The humour is accurate: Quakers would naturally turn to God and most would naturally do that through silence. The silence still stands out as 'unnatural', and in Robert Barclay's words, cannot be counterfeited. Silence thus remains both a defining feature of Quaker worship and a significant outpost of non-worldliness, even in those Quaker groups who are now 'world-accepting'. We return to this idea in Chapter 5.

Chapter 4
Belief

As mentioned in Chapter 1, one of the ways to understand Quaker diversity is to see it in terms of the variety of ways the 1647 experience of Fox, that one, even Christ Jesus could speak to his condition, has been interpreted. The different levels of authority and the meaning given to the experience of direct encounter which is foundational to Quakerism delineates the different groupings of Friends, both historically and in the present day.

The implicit theology of early Friends

One of the frustrations of historians of the first period of Quakerism is the fragmentary and contradictory way in which Quaker theology was presented in the tracts. Terms such as 'Light' and 'Seed' were used in different ways in different places, and whilst Fox was obviously an able and charismatic preacher, he was not a systematic theologian. For these first Friends, it seems that their experience was paramount. Mission too was not based on a theological manifesto as such, but a critique of the rest of Christianity and an appeal to the new possibility inherent in the experience of God breaking into the everyday. Theology is implicit in the early Quaker tracts. Careful research, however, reveals seven recurring themes. Essentially, for early Friends, the inward and continual experience of Christ gave rise to the following key ideas:

1) personal and universal salvation in this life, including the doctrine of perfection;

2) the present and unfolding Second Coming of Christ and the coming of the Kingdom here and now;

3) the apostasy of the rest of Christianity and the way in which Quakers were the true Church;

4) the end of outward sacraments and a separated priesthood, and the use of silence to heighten the sense of presence;

5) scriptural authority as secondary to revelation, but confirming of revelation;

6) witness in the world, including plain dress and plain speech, and also mission;

7) depending on how near at hand Friends felt the Second Coming to be, the need to petition government.

The detail of these arguments was often obscure. In some ways, this set of claims operated from a different place than other Christians. Quakers saw themselves further along the biblical timeline of God's plan for the world, but also, given their critique, of so much, presented the reality of their new covenant in fairly simple terms. Early on they were criticized for playing down the historical Jesus and the Gospels, for over-spiritualizing Christ. In some ways, this was an inevitable consequence of their sense of inward Second Coming. Why focus on the First Coming when the Second was being realized, individually and soon globally? All of their message could be underpinned by scriptural references; they simply didn't always join the dots or join the dots in the same way as each other.

Revelation and scripture

It was Robert Barclay in 1676 and Elizabeth Bathurst in 1679 who first undertook the task of producing a systematic Quaker theology. In their works, *The Apology* and *Truth's Vindication*, respectively, the direct experience of Christ remained central and primary. Theology and witness flowed out from that understanding. Barclay, whose book became influential, as his complete works were published by William Penn after his death, played down the idea of an unfolding Second Coming and modified the doctrine of perfection to allow for those Quakers who fell short. As we saw in Chapters 2 and 3, he used a different argument against outward sacraments. Rather than see the instruction in 1 Cor 1:26 to break the bread until the Lord comes again as anachronistic, he became engaged in an argument over its interpretation. By not framing the Quakers' direct encounter with God within an understanding of the Second Coming, Barclay constructed a meantime theology (which he did by emphasizing the value of peculiarity), and had to deal with the idea of death. Quakers have never had a clear theology of the afterlife because of the early Quaker sense that the Kingdom was to be realized in this one. Barclay maintained the possibility of universal salvation but introduced the possibility of those who rejected or missed God's invitation ('day of visitation') to the new covenant and thus died unregenerate. Barclay also had to work out a theology for those who were awaiting their day of visitation.

Both Fox and Barclay produced Quaker catechisms, but in general Barclay and Bathurst are rare in attempting to produce scholarly renditions of Quaker faith. Quietist writers in the 18th century emphasized the experience of living a life of discernment, of their leadings and concerns, rather than attempting to systematize the theology behind them. Only when it became important to re-present Quakerism to Quakers and to the world did the Evangelical Quakers of the 19th century start to publish these kinds of works, that is, works that attempted to systematize Quaker beliefs, again. The Quietist emphasis on the inward was taken to its logical outcome by some who then disputed the authority of scripture *per se*. At the start of the 19th century, American Friend Hannah Barnard and Abraham Shackleton in Ireland were disowned for questioning scriptural authority. The 'New Lights', as Barnard and her followers were called, challenged the legitimacy and accuracy of scripture when it contradicted their own 'sense' of what God was like. For example, Shackleton and Barnard claimed the Bible could not be inerrant as the God of the New Testament would never support such warlike sentiments as found in the Old Testament. The new evangelical currents in Quakerism were wary of deism and rationalism and keen to promote their new-found version of the Quaker faith. In 1805, Henry Tuke, who had already published *The Faith of the People Called Quakers in Our Lord and Saviour Jesus Christ* in 1801, published his *Principles of Religion, as professed by the Society of Christians, usually called Quakers.* The latter volume went into 12 editions, and it is claimed that by the middle of the century there was hardly a single Quaker home that did not own a copy. It was a book of theology firmly focused on the First Coming of Christ and the propitiatory sacrifice. Fervent Quietists refuted ideas of imputed righteousness and claimed only the *felt* transforming experience of Christ being born within was authentic. In 1806, Philadelphia and Baltimore Yearly Meetings decided that to question the divinity of Jesus or the inerrancy of scripture was a disownable offence. Quakerism was shifting, as we have seen in Chapter 2, but the transition also created a theological debate within the society. This debate has carried on ever since.

The dominant issue was over the interpretation of the inward experience and the level of authority given to that experience in relation to scriptural authority. All else remained shared, including the now firmly meantime understanding of Friends' spirituality. Other tensions, such as over the peculiarities, were common to both sides of the bigger debate. For the Quietists, the inward approach and the knowledge which resulted from that approach was the only authentic basis of spirituality. For Evangelicals, like Gurney, the Inward Light allowed Quakers to read scripture correctly but was not an authority in itself. As we saw in Chapter 2, the debate over the nature and authority of the Inward Light led to the theological aspects of the Great Separation and later the division between Wilburites and Gurneyites.

Once set apart from each other, these different Quaker groups were able to develop their theologies without constraint. Gurneyites emphasized scripture over and above the Inward Light, which some regarded as delusional; Wilburites balanced the experience of the inward Christ with scriptural affirmation; and Hicksites continued to emphasize the experiential and the means to experience as foundational. These, respectively, are the starting points for Evangelical, Conservative, and Liberal Quaker belief today.

Evangelical Quakerism

We saw in Chapter 2 how Gurneyite Quakerism divided into Renewal and Revival tendencies. They held different approaches to the coming of the Kingdom, and different attitudes to the world around them. They also had different views on how important Quakerism was as a distinct witness. However, their theology was largely shared, and division didn't cause a schism but did produce tensions within Evangelical Quakerism. Holiness Quakerism and modernist Quakerism still co-exist within the Evangelical tradition, as does Quakerism influenced by the fundamentalist movement of the early 20th century. Today we can find independent Evangelical Yearly Meetings and those grouped within the umbrella associations of Friends United Meeting (FUM) and Evangelical Friends International (EFI). It is difficult to generalize, but FUM tends to contain predominantly modernist and fundamentalist Meetings, EFI holiness and fundamentalist Meetings. Those Friends drawn towards the outward sacraments are most likely to be within EFI. The degree to which Friends' Churches attempt to operate as community churches or retain Quaker distinctiveness affects the presentation of theology but also the way in which the church is open to new ideas.

Whilst early Friends never held a clear doctrine of the Trinity, the Gurneyite Richmond Declaration of Faith in 1887 began from that understanding:

We believe in one holy, (Isa. 6:3, 58:15) almighty, (Gen. 17:1) all-wise, (Rom. 11:33, 16:27) and everlasting (Ps 90:1–2) God, the Father, (Matt 11:25–27) the Creator (Gen 1:1) and Preserver (Job 7:20) of all things; and in Jesus Christ, His only Son, our Lord, by whom all things were made, (John 1:30) and by whom all things consist; (Col 1:17) and in one Holy Spirit, proceeding from the Father and the Son, (John 15:26, 16:7) the Reprover (John 16:8) of the world, the Witness for Christ, (John 15:26) and the Teacher, (John 14:26) Guide, (John 16:13) and Sanctifier (2 Thess 2:13) of the people of God; and that these three are one in the eternal Godhead; (Matt 28:19, John 10:30, 17:21) to whom be honor, praise, and thanksgiving, now and forever. Amen.

(Faith and Practice of Evangelical
Friends Church Southwest, 2001, p. 27)

In a statement of faith from a Bolivian Evangelical Yearly Meeting, the following points are stressed: God is triune; Christ is divine; the Scriptures have been given by divine inspiration; humanity is sinful; Christ shed His blood as part of an atoning sacrifice; mission is the primary goal of the Church at this time; and Christ will come again and the dead will be resurrected and the faithful saved at God's final Day of Judgement. There may seem to be little difference here from some other Protestant churches, but the differences are in the understandings of the important areas of the nature of the priesthood, the inward sacraments, and of worship. Ecclesiological structures differ too. All of these different interpretations connect back to that foundational experience of 1647. Here, that experience is framed within a Protestant approach to the nature of God, and the divinity and role of Christ:

Northwest Yearly Meeting of Friends Church affirms as essential Christian truths the following teachings: the sovereignty of God; the deity and humanity of Jesus Christ; the atonement through Jesus Christ by which persons are reconciled to God; the resurrection of Jesus, which assures the resurrection of all true worshipers; the gift of the Holy Spirit to believers; and the authority of the Holy Scriptures.

The Yearly Meeting also endorses traditional statements of Friends, including those emphasizing an inward encounter with God, communion without ritual, an individual responsibility for ministry and service, and striving for peace and justice. In addition, the Yearly Meeting speaks to contemporary issues concerning morality, human relationships, and Christian commitment. Friends hold that an authentic Christian belief results in both an inward faith and an outward expression of that belief.

> *(Faith and Practice:*
> *A Book of Christian Discipline, Northwest*
> *Yearly Meeting of Friends Church*, 2003, p. 5)

Christ is central to Evangelical Quaker thinking, as is Christ's role in offering humanity the possibility of salvation through his shed blood:

> We believe that Jesus Christ died on the cross, shedding His blood for us and for our sins and rose again from the dead to make us right with God. A person receives salvation by grace through faith in Jesus Christ as Lord and Savior and not by being good enough to deserve it. To those who receive Christ, God grants forgiveness of sins, the gift of eternal life and ultimately the resurrection of the body to live forever in the new heavens and new earth. Rejecting Jesus Christ and His provisions for salvation and forgiveness of sins results in the penalty of eternal death in hell. The presence of saving faith is revealed by a life lived in obedience to the will of God and results in the good works that God has prepared in advance for us to do.

> (Mylander, 2004, p. 9)

Christ will come again. For some Evangelical Friends, this will be in outward form.

We believe in the Second Coming of our Lord Jesus Christ and all
the great events of the end times prophesied in scripture. We refuse
to divide fellowship over disputed questions of eschatology that are
not clear in the scriptures. We believe in the great resurrection of
both the saved and the lost. We believe everyone will stand before
Christ in the final judgment to receive their just due. Those whose
names are written in the Lamb's book of life will inherit their
eternal rewards in the new heavens and the new earth, freed forever
from selfishness, sin, demonic influence, control and all evil. The
finally unrepentant wicked will suffer the eternal condemnation of
hell prepared for the devil and his angels. At that time Christ will
reign fully over the restored universe and God the Father will be
fully glorified.

(Mylander, 2004, p. 11)

For others, this kind of passage is too literalist or mainstream
and the references to the inward covenant of Jeremiah 31:31–34
remain significant.

Evangelical Quakerism is very broad. This is partly a result
of its huge geographical spread, as well as the cultural and
theological influences of the places where it continues to
grow. It is also to do with choices each Meeting and church
makes about how far to retain distinctive Quaker ideas and
how far to embrace more mainstream Christian thinking.
The decentralized nature of Quakerism adds to the variety of
interpretation.

Conservative Quakerism

Conservative Quakerism is made up of Wilburites, those who
broke away over the introduction of pastoral Quakerism,
and North Carolina Friends, who separated in 1904 over the
introduction of a uniform discipline. In this way, the Conservative
tradition represents an alliance of theological and ecclesiological
conservatism, although also, historically, a mixture of those

happy with Gurneyite formulations of faith and those not. Today Conservative Quakerism can best be described as attempting to conserve Quaker faith and practice, retaining a Christ-centred unprogrammed tradition.

God is assumed, as is Christian belief; the detail is what is left to be explained. In its discipline, North Carolina Yearly Meeting (Conservative) quote George Fox's 1671 letter to the Governor of Barbados. This reads in part:

> ... And we do own and believe that He was made a sacrifice for sin Who knew no sin, neither was guile found in His mouth, and that He was crucified for us in the flesh without the gates of Jerusalem, and that He was buried and that He rose again on the third day by the power of His Father for our justification; and we do believe that He ascended into Heaven and now sitteth on the right hand of God. ... He it is that is now come, and hath given us an understanding that we may know Him that is true. And He rules in our hearts by His law of love and life, and makes us free from the law of sin and death. And we have no life but by Him, for He is the quickening Spirit, the Second Adam, the Lord from Heaven, by Whose blood we are cleansed and our consciences sprinkled from dead works to serve the Living God ...

We do declare that we esteem it a duty incumbent upon us to pray with and for, to teach, instruct and admonish those in and belonging to our families, for whom an account will be required by Him Who comes to judge both quick and dead at the great day of judgment, when every one shall be rewarded according to the deeds done in the body, whether they be good or whether they be evil; at that day we say, of the resurrection both of the good and of the bad, of the just and the unjust: 'When the Lord Jesus shall be revealed from Heaven with His mighty angels, in flaming fire, taking vengeance on them that know not God and obey not the Gospel of our Lord Jesus Christ; who shall be punished with everlasting destruction from the presence of the Lord, and from the glory of

His power, when He shall come to be glorified in his saints, and to be admired in all them that believe in that day. II Thess. 1:7–10; II Peter 3:3.

(*Faith and Practice: Book of Discipline of the North Carolina Yearly Meeting (Conservative) of the Religious Society of Friends*, 1983, pp. 9–11)

This looks like mainstream Christian thinking, but the passage 'He it is that is now come, and hath given us an understanding that we may know Him that is true. And He rules in our hearts by His law of love and life, and makes us free from the law of sin and death' points to a realizing eschatology. The subsequent part of the letter emphasizes the sinful nature of humanity, the continuing wait for justification and sanctification, and ultimately the wait for the Day of Judgement. This is not, then, ultimately, an immediately realizing eschatology, but a meantime experience. But Conservative Friends, like Liberal ones, tend not to dwell on doctrine (see Chapter 5).

The experience of the 'Inner Light,' or the 'Light of Christ,' is the center of the life of Friends and the ultimate source of all our testimonies. The Inner Light is what Friends call 'that of God' in every person which, Friends believe, can be known directly without another's interpretation. The Inner Light gives illumination and clarity to conscience, generating an inward compulsion to follow the leadings of its Spirit. This Spirit is the love of God, implanted in all, overcoming the ambivalence of conscience and leading us to a powerful conviction of God's will for our lives.

The Inner Light is our experience of and connection with God. According to Friends this experience involves a body of convictions about God's nature and His requirements concerning our dealings with all persons. When this body of convictions has consolidated itself in one's inner life and style of outward conduct, it is called 'Truth.' This Truth is a way of following the spirit and not the letter of the law ...

64

... Friends regard their religion in worship and daily life as being guided by the Inner Light. Thus they have no use for dogma and credal formulas. Quakerism can be described but not defined, since it is an inner vision and outward life style rather than a theological world view. It will often be necessary, however, for Friends to relate their experience to that of the Christian community as a whole, and to satisfy this need in a way compatible with the Light which has been given them.

> (*Faith and Practice: Book of Discipline of*
> *the North Carolina Yearly Meeting (Conservative)*
> *of the Religious Society of Friends*, 1983, pp. 6, 9)

The emphasis is on transformation and mutual accountability. The phrase 'Inner Light' came into Quaker currency in the 20th century and is now used more widely than the traditional term, 'Inward Light'.

Liberal Quakerism

Liberal Quakerism, modernist in its rational basis and outlook, became dominant in Britain by about 1905, influenced Renewal Friends in the Evangelical tradition, and developed independently within the Hicksite tradition along a similar time frame. As mentioned in Chapter 2, its key architects were Rufus Jones (himself influenced by, amongst others, John Greenleaf Whittier) and John Wilhelm Rowntree. It was an explicit reaction to both Quietist and Evangelical Quakerism and was constructed on four main ideas:

1) that experience, not scripture, should be primary;

2) that faith should be relevant to the age;

3) that Friends needed to be open to new ideas;

4) that in each age, Friends would know more about the nature and will of God, a doctrine called 'progressivism', and that, as such, revelation has a chronological authority.

14. John Greenleaf Whittier (1807–92)

These Liberal Friends wanted to retain a distinctive Quakerism rooted in the experience of the direct encounter and yet not return to the Quietistic peculiarities.

Christianity was assumed rather than prescribed. In Britain, the 1921 Book of Discipline replaced the section on 'Christian Doctrine' with one entitled 'Illustrative Spiritual Experiences of Friends'. This approach to theology is discussed in the next chapter, but this was symbolic of a shift to pure experience away from one affirmed by particular scriptural understandings. Indeed, the set of ideas listed above meant that, theologically, this form of Quakerism was not tied to any text or any tradition. Implicit within it was the Whig optimism of the period and the sense that the future equated to progress. The London Yearly Meeting in 1931 urged Friends to be 'open to new light from whatever quarter', and the question as to whether Quakerism was necessarily Christian was repeatedly raised on both sides of the Atlantic in the decade that followed.

By the 1960s, possibly enhanced by a growing trend for Quakers converting into the group rather than growing up in the faith, non-Christian Quakers were part of the Liberal tradition. Two world wars, the Holocaust, the dropping of atomic bombs, war in Korea and South East Asia, gave ample if unwanted opportunity for Quakers to express their testimony against war and to be publicly identified as counter-cultural. Within the Liberal tradition, the emphasis on experience allowed those with less-defined faith or clearly non-Christian ideas, but drawn by this testimony, to find a place within Quakerism.

Present-day Liberal Quakerism is highly permissive of differing belief systems and there are, for example, Muslim, Hindu, Buddhist, and non-theist Quakers within Liberal Yearly Meetings.

In recent surveys, just over 72% of British Quakers said they believed in God, with a further 24% saying they were 'not sure'. In surveys offering a simple 'yes/no' response, most of these 'agnostics' claimed they too believed in God. However, the interpretation of what 'God' means or may be varies enormously. The emphasis on experience accommodates a diversity of interpretation. Bible use is low, and the Bible is considered by most British Friends as an optional part of their spirituality. Consequent to that is a highly varied approach to Jesus/Christ. Asked if Jesus is an important figure in their spiritual life, 39% of British Quakers replied in the affirmative. A further 32% claimed 'it varies'. Jesus was 'best described' as 'a spiritual teacher' by nearly 70% of the same sample. Jesus as 'Christ, the son of God' achieved a 13% response in a straight yes/no question.

These figures contrast hugely with the Evangelical Quaker tradition and the quotations above. Christianity is now an option within Liberal Quakerism and, as such, ideas of the Second Coming are rarely voiced. For many, there is no First Coming, let alone the promise of second one. Ideas of sin and salvation are also rarely mentioned. One of the few references to sin and salvation in the British Book of Discipline reads as follows:

> Directly I admit that my life might be better than it is. I have a sense of failure and feel a need of help from something or someone outside myself. This sense and this need are to me the meanings of the terms 'sense of sin' and 'need of salvation'.

> (*Quaker Faith and Practice*, 1995: 26.10)

The use of the 'Inner Light' instead of 'Inward Light' has led some Liberal Friends to adopt ideas of a residual divinity within everyone, and original blessings (after Matthew Fox) rather than original sin. 'Light' is used widely, but interpreted individually. The early and various Quaker use of the term 'Light' allows Liberal Friends to avoid doctrinal specificity.

The Light Within is the fundamental and immediate experience for Friends. It is that which guides each of us in our everyday lives and brings us together as a community of faith. It is, most importantly, our direct and unmediated experience of the Divine.

> *(Faith and Practice: A Book of*
> *Christian Discipline, Philadelphia Yearly Meeting*
> *of the Religious Society of Friends*, 2002, p. 16)

The Light operates inwardly, hence the continued emphasis on unprogrammed worship, but Liberal Friends do not need to corporately specify its theological nature or character. The North Pacific Yearly Meeting make this clear in the following passage:

One central area of belief which has received considerable attention over the years is the relationship of Quakerism to Christianity. Whether one interprets the Quaker movement as a strand within Protestantism or as a third force distinct from both Protestantism and Catholicism, the movement, both in its origin and in the various branches which have evolved, is rooted in Christianity. However, from its inception it has offered both a critique of many accepted manifestations of Christianity and an empathy with people of faith beyond the bounds of Christianity. Some Friends have placed particular emphasis on the Gospel of Jesus Christ, while others have found more compelling a universal perspective emphasizing the Divine Light enlightening every person. One of the lessons of our own history as a religious movement is that an excessive reliance on one or the other of these perspectives, neglecting the essential connectedness between the two, has been needlessly divisive and has drawn us away from the vitality of the Quaker vision at its best.

In yearly meetings such as ours, the concern of Friends is not that members affirm a particular verbal formulation of this faith but that it be a living and transforming power within their lives. Challenged by the words of Jesus as quoted in Matthew 7:21 – 'It is

not those who say to me, "Lord, Lord," who will enter the kingdom
of heaven, but those who do the will of my Father in heaven' – we
do not place emphasis on the naming of God. Instead we encourage
one another, in John Woolman's phrase, 'to distinguish the
language of the pure Spirit which inwardly moves upon the heart.'
In the course of following this spiritual path, many Friends do come
to find great depths of meaning in familiar Christian concepts and
language, while others do not.

(*Faith and Practice*,
North Pacific Yearly Meeting, 1993, p. 12)

The experience of direct encounter remains central, but in
the Liberal tradition it has been reframed within a pluralist
context. Diversity is celebrated. It is experience and the means to
experience which are given prominence in this tradition. In other
words, Liberal Quakerism is not defined in terms of doctrine but
in terms of the form of Quakerism, the way in which the Quaker
group is Quaker, its worship and business method, its testimony
and values. Belief is plural but also marginal. Ask a Liberal
Quaker what they believe and the answer typically includes a
list of statements about worship, such as 'we don't sing hymns,
we don't have a separated priesthood, we don't have outward
sacraments'. It can feel like an evasion to the eager enquirer, but
these Friends are simply answering the question on their own
terms: this is what is central to our faith, that is, the way we
worship – the means to experience.

Thus, whilst some Friends, particularly those who feel
Quakerism needs to be Christian, have grieved at the growing
diversity, Liberal Quakers are held together by a strong adherence
to its distinctive form of worship and business and to its
testimony and values. Where Quakers are non-theist, the business
method is simply reinterpreted. They are also bound together by a
particular attitude to theology and language, explored in the next
chapter.

Summary

The question of belief is given different prominence and different levels of specificity across the three main traditions of Quakerism. For Evangelical Friends, whilst worship practice can vary, belief is central and definitional and can be clearly delineated. Conservative Friends also have a fairly narrow band of belief but place less emphasis on it as a discrete category. They are more concerned with the experience of worship as a primary category. This emphasis on worship is true too of Liberal Friends, but in this tradition, belief is plural and includes the non-Christian and non-theist. There is a conformist attitude to form within the Liberal tradition and permissive attitude to belief.

Chapter 5
Theology and language

This chapter considers the very distinctive approach Quakers have traditionally taken regarding language and how it has been adapted by the different kinds of Quakerism we find in the world today. In particular, the chapter focuses on the use of silence in the Liberal Quaker tradition and their caution around theology.

Early Quakers, language, and theology

In Chapter 3, we explored how the first Quakers rationalized and used silence as a medium through which to approach God. This was a worship method borrowed from the Seekers, but it was also affirmed by reference to Revelation. In their critique of the outward, early Quakers were wary of 'carnal talk' and of 'fleshly speaking', of 'idle words' (after Matthew 12:36). 'Natural language' had come into being at Babel and was not part of the Edenic state Friends felt they had returned to – there, they could comprehend God without outward tongue. This was the inward covenant written on their hearts after Jeremiah 31, 'No longer shall they teach one another, or say to each other, "Know the LORD," for they shall all know me' (Jeremiah 31:34).

Where Protestantism had interiorized much ritual, Quakers took it a step further with their interiorization of the Word (the

experience of Christ). Silence was about both the stopping of
that which needed to be silenced, as well as a reverential and
unencumbered state for the encounter with Christ. It was both
a closing down of the old life and an opening up to God's Word
and the new life. It was both a consequence of experience and a
means to it. Ultimately, it was concerned with the revelation and
realization of the Kingdom.

Where outward speech was used, it was to advocate this silencing
of self and will.

> Now, thou must die in the silence, to the fleshly wisdom,
> knowledge, reason, and understanding ... Keep to that of God in
> you which will lead you up to God, when you are still from your own
> thoughts, and imaginations, and desires and counsels of your own
> hearts, and motions, and will; when you stand single from all these,
> waiting upon the Lord, your strength is renewed.
>
> (Fox, 1990, vol. 4, p. 132)

Silence was the means to worship and to inward communion.
Speech needed to come out of that silence, that place of
communion, and work to gather the other worshippers further
into that spiritual space. Silence was the means to God, the means
to ministry, the basis of ministry, and the means through which
ministry was received – both the basis and the consequence of
speech. In other words, it was the way to be open to speech, to
test whether it was ministry, and the way to hear ministry. At a
Meeting at Preston Patrick in 1652, Fox was expected to speak
early on in the gathering but only did so when 'led', in spite of the
anxiety of those who had organized the event. Speech was from
God, could not be bidden or organized or programmed. Given
the desire to die to the self in worship and avoid will-worship,
the speaker was defined as entirely passive, merely a channel for
the Word of God (Ezekial 3:27; Ezekial 33:22; Matthew 10:20).
Richard Farnsworth wrote in 1663:

15. Quaker Meeting in Philadelphia, 19th century

And as the bodies of men and women subjected unto and guided by the spirit of God are the temple of God; therefore the Spirit of God may speak in and through them; and as the Lord is the teacher of his people he may be the speaker in them and through them.

(Bauman, 1983, p. 25)

In these ways, Quaker talk in the 1650s was spiritualized, deemed to come from beyond the speaker. Small talk or worldly talk was seen as superfluity and inappropriate. Thus, from the very beginnings, Quakers were wary of saying too much, but most importantly, were concerned to make sure what they did say came from the right place. As we have seen in Chapter 3, this is still a primary concern for those who minister in open worship. Later conventions, about length and frequency of ministry, protect the silence from misuse and help remind Friends that the ministry they give is not theirs, but God's.

As well as preformed modes of worship, the early Friends were also highly concerned about a theology built on 'notions' – profession without possession. The experience of God breaking into their lives had given them new insight into the empty forms and words of other Christians. As Fox concluded, reflecting on his 1647 experience, all were 'shut up in unbelief' as he had been, even whilst they claimed, as he had, to be good Christians. Only the direct experience of Christ released the believer from captivity. Margaret Fell's convincement carried a similar message, that the inward was authentic, and that erstwhile reliance on the outward had been a deception.

In the year 1652 it pleased the Lord to draw him [George Fox] toward us ... My then husband, Thomas Fell, was not at home at that time, but gone the Welsh circuit, being one of the Judges of Assize, and our house [Swarthmoor Hall] being a place open to entertain ministers and religious people at, one of George Fox his friends brought him hither, where he stayed all night. And the next day, being a lecture or a fast-day, he went to Ulverston steeplehouse, but came not in till people were gathered; I and my children had been a long time there before. And when they were singing before the sermon, he came in; and when they had done singing, he stood up upon his seat or form and desired that he might have liberty to speak. And he that was in the pulpit said he might. And the first words that he spoke were as followeth: 'He is not a Jew that is one outward, neither is that circumcision which is outward, but he is a Jew that is one inward, and that is circumcision which is of the heart'. And so he went on and said, How that Christ was the Light of the world and lighteth every man that cometh into the world; and that by this Light they might be gathered to God, etc. And I stood up in my pew, and I wondered at his doctrine, for I had never heard such before. And then he went on, and opened the Scriptures, and said, 'The Scriptures were the prophets' words and Christ's and the apostles' words, and what as they spoke they enjoyed and possessed and had it from the Lord'. And said, 'Then what had any to do with the Scriptures, but as they came to the Spirit that gave them forth. You will say, Christ saith this, and the apostles say this; but what canst thou say? Art thou a child of Light and hast walked in the Light, and what thou speakest is it inwardly from God?'

This opened me so that it cut me to the heart; and then I saw clearly we were all wrong. So I sat me down in my pew again, and cried bitterly. And I cried in my spirit to the Lord, 'We are all thieves, we are all thieves, we have taken the Scriptures in words and know nothing of them in ourselves' ... I saw it was the truth, and I could not deny it; and I did as the apostle saith, I 'received the truth in the love of it'. And it was opened to me so clear that I had never a tittle in my heart against it; but I desired the Lord that I might be kept in it, and then I desired no greater portion.

(*Quaker Faith and Practice*, 1995: 19.07)

Once revealed, Friends had to share this knowledge, for everyone else was shut up in unbelief, or a 'thief'.

Thus, these Quakers critiqued the outward as it impacted on worldly speech but also on 'empty' theology which was not rooted in the experience of the direct encounter with God. This did not turn them into a silent order or one which avoided all theology; it was the authenticity of speech and theology that mattered. Creeds have been a particular focus of the Quaker critique of formulaic and inauthentic theology over the centuries.

Present-day attitudes to theology and language

What we find in the present-day traditions are variations on the early Quaker position, albeit ones linked back in some ways to this original stance. The Evangelical tradition, where it has moved closer to the Protestant mainstream, has abandoned aspects of the early Quaker critique of outward forms and times and seasons, whilst still claiming that worship and speech are spirit-led. Gurneyite Yearly Meetings agreed a Declaration of Faith at Richmond in 1887, which whilst not a creed reads very much like one, as the opening passage quoted in Chapter 4 shows.

The degree to which it is enforced has led to tension and division in the 20th century. The Conservative tradition appears closest to the early Quaker position.

> As Friends so affirm and seek an ever more perfect openness to that Guidance in their daily lives, they have found it preferable to offer no allegiance to either doctrine, dogma, or creed.
>
> (*Faith and Practice: Book of Discipline of the North Carolina Yearly Meeting (Conservative) of the Religious Society of Friends*, 1983, pp. 6, 9)

The Liberal tradition has turned a caution over speech and empty theology into a caution over theological speech, as we see below.

Another way of looking at these present-day variations over the authority given theology is in terms of realism, semi-realism, and non-realism – the degree to which the experience of God and what we can say about that experience are deemed true. Early Friends were 'realist', that is, they believed their experience of God was real and that their theology was true. What they had to say about God and the relationship between humanity and the divine was accurate and correct. This is also an accurate description of most present-day Evangelical and Conservative Friends. When Evangelical Friends present their theology (again, see Chapter 4 for some examples), they are clear that they are right about it and that the words match the reality. Liberal Friends are non-realist, or, more typically, semi-realist.

Non-realists suggest that religious belief symbolizes our highest human ideals and that such belief does not refer to anything 'real' (hence the term 'non-realist'). This idea is similar to the German philosopher Ludwig Feuerbach's view of 'God' as the summation of humanity's political aspirations, and lends affirmation to the writings of the Anglican Don Cupitt and the Sea of Faith movement, in which some Quakers are very active.

From a realist point of view, the statement 'God exists' is either true or false. Statements made about God are like statements made about your car: they either correspond to reality, the 'facts' or they don't. But, says Cupitt, there's another way of looking at all this: a nonrealist way. From this viewpoint, God is understood not as a real person, power or entity (an intelligence, an energy, a thing like a rock or a daisy) but as a symbol or as an idea. God is a fiction, but a necessary, instrumental fiction.

(Boulton, 2002, p. 149)

In this version of Quakerism, a realist God is unnecessary, inappropriate, or just plain wrong.

However, within the Liberal tradition, an implicit semi-realist position is dominant. God, or 'God', is real but statements about God are not facts about God but interpretations of the experience of God. Indeed, in a paradoxical way, the non-realist statements about God are more certain in their conviction than the semi-realists. Semi-realists believe that the experience of God is real but that theological statements cannot get close to describing the mystery of the Divine. In this sense, theology is not ultimately 'real' or true in anything other than a symbolic sense. Beliefs are held to be 'true' personally, partially, or provisionally, but not true for everyone for all time. This is based on a criticism of the ability of humanity and of language to describe adequately religious and spiritual experience rather than any critique of God. Theology for most Liberal Friends is clearly 'empirically unverifiable':

> ... statements about 'God' are better approached as models rather than truths... Since no ultimate truth can be known by definition, religion is about commitment based on open-minded enquiry, not belief.

(Punshon, 1989, p. 27)

Semi-realists are not necessarily questioning the existence of something beyond the material. It is simply that their implicit diversity of explanation and expression tends towards a pluralism of belief. In this way, the 'something beyond the material' becomes variously described and part of a permissive belief system. God is variously and alternatively described and God's attributes vary between Quakers. This semi-realism forms part of a particular Liberal Quaker approach to theology, which itself is accommodated by the historic value given silence and the caution over speech. This phenomenon is explored in greater detail below.

Liberal Quakers and theology

The original Liberal Quaker emphasis on experience was founded partly on a critique of Evangelical Quakerism and in part a rationalist foundation that wanted to accommodate and circumvent the findings of higher criticism and biblical scholarship of the late Victorian age. As explained in Chapter 4, the combination of pure experience and progressivism and the injunction to be open to new ideas allowed Liberal Quakerism enormous freedom to explore new ways of thinking about God and new ways of thinking about theology. By the late 20th century, a distinctive approach to language and theology had developed.

As we have seen in Chapter 3, silence is highly valued. As for the early Friends, it is the means to experience, and the consequence of experience. Superficially, silence marks the boundaries of the collective worship. It is also the medium through which God's will is heard, voiced, and discerned.

It is through the silence, then, that:

1) God is experienced by the individual and, thus, the individual authority for belief in God is given;
2) the silent approach is validated through the fact that participants claim they experience God in the silence;

3) 'God's will' is discerned by the individual through 'leadings';
4) ideas of what might constitute God's will are shared and 'tested' in worship;
5) action consequent to God's will is agreed upon in Business Meetings, based in silent worship;
6) the appointment of those to carry out the work are considered and made in Business Meetings based in silent worship.

Silence and its use are crucial to the way the Quaker group operates. At the same time, speech is devalued as a consequence of the theological role given collective silence. The status of speech is also diminished as a result of the popular semi-realist Quaker view on a) the possibility, and b) the appropriateness, of speech to communicate belief. Firstly, words are not seen to be of practical use in expressing spirituality. Words are merely blunt guesses at the truth.

> ... God *an sich* is an utterly unknowable X and that what we cannot speak about, of that we must remain silent! Theology is richer and not poorer for this silence.

> (Leichty, 1990, p. 83)

Secondly, Liberal Quakers claim it is not appropriate to try and verbalize religious belief. This view is based on the premise that the nature of language and the nature of God are qualitatively distinct. Coherence takes the believer away from God: what looks exact and clear is likely to be wrong. Language limits the understanding of God.

> Quakerism is a group of insights, attitudes, and practices which together form a way of life, rather than a dogma or creed. It rests on a conviction that by looking into their inmost hearts people can have a direct communion with their Creator. This experience cannot ultimately be described in words, but Quakers base their whole lives on it.

> (*The Quaker Way*, 1998)

At one level, God and the experience of God are inexpressible.

> God cannot be fitted into preformed notions bounded by expression
> in words. Faith must allow for elements of radical unknowability
> and mystery about God.
>
> (Hewitt, 1990, p. 757)

Quaker theology is then necessarily minimalistic. In some ways,
silence is a more accurate response to theological questions than
speech. In this sense, Liberal Quakers set themselves apart from
either a text-centric or oral tradition.

> For many of us, I feel sure, putting 'God' into words at all is to
> trivialise the very thing we are seeking to convey ... the silence of
> meeting means so much to me. Where else can I go to share with
> others what is beyond words?
>
> (Letter to *The Friend* (1992), 150, p. 471)

In these ways, vocal expression of belief is devalued. By inference
(as in the 17th century), the free ministry is properly concerned
with that which is beyond words. In the 20th century, not just
God but theology itself came to be seen as inexpressible (a shift
from the 17th century).

The lack of a vocal confession of faith, or a structural
requirement to subscribe to any set of words, allows silence
on matters of belief to continue. In the past, the invisibility of
belief would not have been problematic: Friends had a greater
unity over matters of belief and could assume knowledge of
each other's theology; and there was less fear of isolation, due to
the wider use of religious language. There is a hesitation about
expressing theology in or out of Meeting. For a group in which
the theological norm is invisible but a potentially sensitive issue,
keeping quiet involves less risk than sharing belief. Present-day
British Quakerism contains a theological diversity which has

emerged under the cover of silence and which remains unchecked and uncheckable and partly unknown. The process operates in the following way:

1) Worship and the use of silence is the basis of Quaker form. Quaker religious experience occurs within the silence, and types of individual belief are constructed to help make sense of that experience.

2) Theological belief may be vocalized in ministry but frequently is not, either through a lack of opportunity or lack of courage (with the silence used as a form of self-censor or defence against creating conflict).

3) The lack of vocalization of belief means that there is no reaction.

4) The silence operates at this stage of the process as a consequence of a) silence used as a form of worship, and b) silence used as a defence.

5) In this way, changes to popular belief, as newcomers enter the group or as participants change the language of their theology, occur covertly.

> There are those who will say that our unity lies in the silence of our meetings for worship, a silence beyond words and ideas. That silence can also be used as a cloak to cover up and smother our disunity, in which nothing considered 'divisive' can be uttered or done.
>
> (Letter to *The Friend* (1992), 150, p. 604)

Whilst the form of worship operates as a means of cohesion to the group, its varying interpretations could at some stage begin to unpick the form. The Meeting for Worship for business, for example, also based in silence, has traditionally been seen as a means to the discernment of the will of God. For those without a God or a God with a will, this formula is anachronistic. Instead, for these Friends, the business method is a temperamental or political preference. This may be a challenge up ahead in the Liberal tradition.

For those who are more thoroughly realist in terms of belief and theology, the majority of Friends worldwide, Liberal Quaker diversity can look like a supermarket religion, a pick-and-mix approach. The loss of an accepted and assumed Christianity is confusing and bewildering to Evangelical and Conservative Friends. Self-led eclecticism can appear an overly diffuse form of religion. What is often misunderstood by Friends in these other traditions is that, whilst this may be true, belief is not central to Liberal Friends. It is not how Liberal Friends define their Quakerism, but rather, and merely, an attempt to explain the nature of their *experience*, which is primary. Liberal Friends emphasize the form of Quakerism not because they don't believe anything but because it is the form that leads to the experience, which for them is central (see Chapter 4). This position, however, is alien to Evangelical Quakers.

Moreover, Liberal Quakerism is now bounded, beyond the theological diversity, and the coherence around form, by a particular approach to theologizing, what I have termed 'the absolute perhaps'. In other words, Liberal Quakerism is held together by *how* it believes. The set of characteristics that founded Liberal Quakerism and allowed it to be forever on the move have become normative. Not only can Friends be open to new ideas and new revelation, but now they should be. The possibility of seeking in multiple directions and subsequent pluralism and difference within the group has become a norm and a boundary.

The ideas of progressivism and of being open to new Light have become translated into the notion that the group cannot know Truth, except personally, partially, or provisionally. Thus Liberal Quakerism is not just about the possibility of seeking, it is about the certainty of never finally finding. Liberal Friends can seek anywhere where they are sure they will not find. All theology is 'towards', a 'perhaps' kind of exercise. In a rational philosophical understanding of the nature of religion, these Friends have decided that religious truth claims are problematic, neither true nor false but rationally meaningless. From outside the religious enterprise they are sure of this. In other words, they are absolutely certain (rationally) that they can never be certain (theologically). They operate a doctrine of the 'absolute perhaps', and they operate it in a prescriptive way. In other words, these Friends are zealous, even fundamentalist, about their theological stance of corporate uncertainty. The non-realists, in their certainty, sit uneasily within a Liberal tradition currently based on a principle of theological 'perhapsness'. Like Christian Quakers who feel they have been 'eldered' for their theology, non-realist Friends have sometimes misunderstood their discomfort in terms of theological tension rather than an epistemological tension. Those who find theological truth or who wish to share it with the rest of the group, such as the non-realists, feel uncomfortable. One of the ironies for such a permissive group is that the Liberal Quaker position holds that any group or any individual who claims to have found the final truth, for all people or for all time, is wrong. Whilst other believers may sometimes be uncertain about elements of the certainty of their Church's confession, Liberal Quakers are certain that they can only be uncertain. According to Liberal Quakerism, all religious groups have to be at least partly wrong theologically.

So, ecumenically, Liberal Quakers are in an interesting position. They believe in a very different way from most religious groups. First, they hold belief as a category in very different esteem but, second, they also tend to judge down all those groups who place belief as central and who think theology can be or is true. The 'absolute perhaps' is the defining characteristic of the Liberal Quaker and is the key difference between these Friends and the whole of the rest of Quakerism, worldwide today and historically. These other Quakers are perhaps or absolute about their absolutes, realist, and far less cautious about maintaining a corporate theology (see Chapter 7).

All of the Quaker traditions treat language slightly differently from the first Friends. Evangelicals and Conservatives and Liberals are less concerned about 'carnal talk', but Liberal Friends have been the most innovative in the area of theology, replacing a concern about worldly talk with a concern about theology itself.

Chapter 6
Ecumenism

Quaker perspectives on ecumenism, the ways in which they work
with other Churches and faiths, have varied widely over time.
In particular, they have varied in line with the degree to which
Quakers have seen themselves as the one true Church. Their
ecumenical outlook has also been framed partly by how close they
felt the Second Coming and Day of Judgement to be. This chapter
explores these variations and uses British Quakerism as a case
study of some of the challenges facing Liberal Friends in their
ecumenical partnerships.

The 1650s

In the 1650s, Quakers as co-agents with God as the vanguard of
the new dispensation had little time for believers of other types
and in particular for those who led them. At the same time,
the sense of unfolding endtime gave this critique an urgency,
contributing to its zeal.

Benjamin Nicholson's *A Brief Discovery of the Three-Fold Estate
of Antichrist*, published in 1653, was a particularly strong barrage
against the state Church. The reverence for church buildings, the
rule of clergy, and the state-sponsored parish system were the
principal targets of the tract. It is particularly strident against
the clergy, who, it claimed, mystified the people and robbed them

of authentic spirituality: 'Howle ye proud priests, the Lord is coming ... you must be called to account ... Your kingdom must be taken from you ... Repent, repent, and give over deceiving of the people, and make restitution to whom you have robbed' (Gwyn, 1995, p. 138).

In Edward Burrough's 1656 tract, *A Trumpet of the Lord Sounded Forth Out of Sion*, God, through the pen of Burrough, takes 23 different individuals and groups to task. Amongst them are 'all the Priests, and Prophets, and Teachers of the People'. It is their deceit and hypocrisy which is particularly abhorrent.

> For you in hypocrisie, and deceit, and abominations, hath exceeded all other that ever went before you, and are less excusable than they, and more vile in my sight ... abominable and loathsome and heinous, is your filthinesse in preaching for hire, and for gifts, and rewards, and in making a prey upon the people ... you have not stood in my counsel, but have erred from my way ... you have shut the kingdom of heaven against men, to the destruction of thousands, and ten thousands who have perished under your ministry, whom you have caused to erre, and led them out of the way ... it was your generation of the same seed that put the Apostles to death and now you make merchandize of their words.
>
> (Burrough, 1656, pp. 10–11)

Apostasy was one thing, but apostasy which then prevented others from being part of this new covenant, purely out of selfish motivation, was considered heinous. This kind of Quaker invective was common in the 1650s.

The first Friends held a doctrine of universal salvation and believed that all could come to Christ regardless of their carnal knowledge of scripture. This was not an incipient universalism but a keen sense that all could and should become Quakers and enjoy the spiritual intimacy with the one true God that they did.

Christ hath enlightened every man that comes into the world, he hath enlightened the Turks, Jews, and Moors, with the light, (which is the life in him the word,) that all in the light might know God and Christ; and 'the grace of God which brings salvation hath appeared unto all men;' so to the Turks, Jews, and Moors, yea, to all nations; so that with the grace of God they may be taught to deny ungodliness and unrighteousness, and live righteously and godly; and therefore all must come to this grace of God in their hearts, which brings their salvation, (if they have salvation,) and come to the throne of grace; and this is the covenant of grace, in which is the election; and God, who made all, pours out of his spirit upon all men and women in the world, in the days of his new covenant, yea, upon whites and blacks, Moors, and Turks, and Indians, Christians, Jews, and Gentiles, that all with the spirit of God, might know God and the things of God, and serve and worship him in his spirit and truth, that he hath given them. But they that do resist the truth, and quench, and vex, and grieve, and rebel against the spirit that God hath given them, such are not like to serve and worship God in his spirit and truth; but he that endures to the end in God's grace, spirit, light, and truth, shall be saved.

(Epistle 388, Fox 1990, Vol. 8)

Everyone was the same. Everyone had the chance to accept God's invitation to the new life and salvation, or to resist and grieve. Margaret Fell wrote four tracts to the Jews of Holland and was an advocate of their readmission to England (Jews had been expelled in 1295). These tracts were carefully crafted in the language of the Hebrew Bible, but their aim was to turn Jews from their outward observances to the 'pure law of God in your hearts' and to convert the Jews to the Quaker experience and to help usher in the coming of the Kingdom:

Therefore, Israel, arise and shine, for thy Light is come, and the Glory of the Lord is risen upon thee ... so this is the Day of Visitation: awake, awake, stand up of Jerusalem.

(Fell, 1710 [1656], p. 110)

Thus, the first period of Quakerism was not universalist or ecumenical, and neither was it polite. When John Luffe met Pope Alexander VII, he spoke 'truth to power':

> Thou pretendest to sit in Peter's chair,' said Luffe according to this account. 'Now know that Peter had no chair but a boat: Peter was a fisher, thou art a Prince: Peter fasted and prayed, thou farest deliciously and sleepest softly: he was mean in attire, thou art beset with ornaments and gay attire: he fished for men to convert them, thou hookest souls to confound them: he was a friend and disciple to Christ, thou art indeed Antichrist.
>
> (Braithwaite, 1912, p. 424)

Luffe was hung the morning after this exchange. In Boston, as mentioned in Chapter 1, the Puritan rulers of the colony hanged

16. **Quaker Mary Dyer led to execution i**[...]usetts Bay Colony, 1659

four Quakers, including Mary Dyer, for their beliefs. The lack of ecumenical spirit ran both ways and created the first Quaker martyrs.

The Restoration

In the 1660s, as with so much else, Quakers modified their outlook towards other groups in that they worked with others to seek relief from persecution and religious toleration. By 1662, the Quaker message towards the priests and professors was tempered.

All Nations have been vailed under the clouds of the Night of Apostacy; although there hath been a profession of God and Christ, and a form of Worship hath been set up, yet the Power of God hath been wanting, and the Life of Jesus Christ hath not been known amongst them; such have had the *Form of Godliness*, but have denied the *Power of God*, which maketh able to overcome all things contrary unto God: But the reason why the Power of God hath not been known, to the overcoming of Sin and Uncleaness amongst Professors, they have not been in that in which Power is given from God, ... And all Professors at this day must come unto the Corner-stone, to be fitted and squared thereby for the building up of the Spiritual house; and every stone of the building of God must be living, like unto the Corner-stone; and all must come unto the Light of the perfect day, that the perfection of Beauty they may come to behold, that the Glory of all Nations may shine amongst you.

(White, 1662)

Priests still 'out of the power of the Lord' but could choose to be 'fitted and squared', to be part of the coming Kingdom. After the 1 Quakers were less hostile to other religious groups. As the meantime bece of the Second Coming receded, living in the the immediate e ongoing reality and surviving persecution publish a tract a cond Day's Morning Meeting refused to e Baptists in 1674 because 'as the Case

now stands between the Bapts & Friends They would not willingly
have other Controversyes brought in to make more worke' (Reay,
1985, p. 111). Barclay, in his *Apology*, was highly critical of the
notions of other Christians but tellingly, at the very end of his long
and forceful passage against outward sacraments, he stops short
of a total condemnation of all those who worship in that way.
Instead, he claims:

> Lastly, if any now at this day, from a true tenderness of spirit, and
> with real conscience towards God, did practice this ceremony in
> the same way, method, and manner as did the primitive Christians,
> recorded in Scripture (which yet none, that I know, now do) I
> should not doubt to affirm, but they might be indulged in it, and
> the Lord might regard them, and for a season appear to them, in
> the use of these things, as many of us have known him to do to us
> in the time of our ignorance, providing always they did not seek
> to obtrude them upon others, nor judge such, as found themselves
> delivered, or that they do not pertinaciously adhere to them. For we
> certainly know that the day is dawned, in which God hath arisen
> and hath dismissed all those ceremonies and rites, and is only to
> be worshipped in Spirit, and that he appears to them who wait
> upon him, and that to seek God in these things is, with Mary at
> the sepulchre, to seek the living among the dead, for we know that
> he is risen and revealed in Spirit, leading his children out of these
> rudiments, that they may walk with him in his Light: to whom be
> glory for ever. Amen.
>
> (prop. 13, Barclay, 2002)

Sincere error is taken into account by God, as God had already
shown with the Quakers. As long as those in error did not force
others to take part in anachronistic ritual, 'The Lord might regard
them'. Barclay, of course, needed to end with a reaffirmation of
the Quaker position that 'the day is dawned'. But, as we have seen
above, what Barclay meant by this new Day was different from
Fox. This passage is another example of the changes that took
place within Quakerism after 1660.

17. The Seal of Penn's Colony, 'Pennsilvania'

When William Penn set up the Holy Experiment in Pennsylvania, religious toleration and peace were its two key ideals, a symbol, more than anything else, of how far Quaker ecumenism had developed, or could develop given political freedom. Rhode Island too, under Quaker control, promised liberty of conscience. Section 35 of the Frame of Government for Pennsylvania read:

> That all persons living in this Province, who confess and
> acknowledge the One Almighty and Eternal God, to be the Creator,
> Upholder and Ruler of the World, and that hold themselves obliged
> in Conscience to live peaceably and justly in Civil Society, shall in
> no wayes be molested or prejudiced for their Religious Perswasion
> or Practice in matters of Faith and Worship, nor shall they be
> compelled at any time to frequent or maintain any Religious
> Worship, Place or Ministry whatever.

(Dunn and Dunn, 1982, p. 225)

This is a very generous accommodation of diversity enshrined in a principle of liberty of conscience. Albeit in a different context, this is a stark contrast to the first years of the movement.

The 18th and 19th centuries

Whilst a sectarian outlook characterized the 'familied monasticism' of the 18th century, life in 'the world' inevitably led to increasing contact with other Christians. Areas of common concern amongst nonconformists gave rise to work held in common.

Witness against the slave trade in the late 18th century both fed and was fed by an increasing sense of unity between Quakers influenced by the Evangelical Revival and evangelicals in other traditions. Quietists were also opposed to the slave trade but less open to working with the 'world's people'. For Evangelical Quakers, 'the world' was now only those outside of Christianity. Joseph John Gurney addressed the British and Foreign Bible

OBSERVATIONS

On the Inflaving, importing and purchaſing of

Negroes;

With ſome Advice thereon, extracted from the Epiſtle of the Yearly-Meeting of the People called QUAKERS, held at *London* in the Year 1758.

Anthony Benezet

When ye ſpread forth your Hands, I will hide mine Eyes from you, yea when ye make many Prayers I will not hear; your Hands are full of Blood. Waſh ye, make you clean, put away the Evil of your Doings from before mine Eyes Iſai. 1, 15.

Is not this the Faſt that I have choſen, to looſe the Bands of Wickedneſs, to undo the heavy Burden, to let the Oppreſſed go free, and that ye break every Toke, Chap. 58, 7.

Second Edition.

GERMANTOWN:
Printed by CHRISTOPHER SOWER. 1760.

18. Title page of Anthony Benezet, *Observations on the Inslaving, Importing and Purchasing of Negroes* (1760)

Society on the extent to which non-religious people could be allowed to help the work, not on any challenges of Christian unity. As for Gurney himself, whilst tempted to become an Anglican, as many Quakers were, he experienced a strong sense that God wanted him, following Quaker tradition, to keep his hat on when greeting his hosts at two high society dinners. He followed this 'leading' and claimed he found himself, and was understood by others, to be a 'decided Quaker'.

Evangelical Friends such as Gurney began to see Quakerism as part of the true Christian Church, rather than the sole true Church. Gurney began his *Observations On The Distinguishing Views & Practices Of The Society Of Friends* (1979 [1824]) with the evident grounds of unity between Christians, before addressing the Quaker distinctives. It is a Gurneyite Quaker version of the essentials of Christianity but it still contrasts, for example, with Barclay's tone and stance. However, similarly to Barclay, whilst Gurney believed Friends were correct in their interpretation of scripture, he ended the chapter in *Observations* on communion in an ecumenical spirit, asking Friends not to judge those who continue these practices, as God accepts the sincere heart and 'is pleased to bless a variety of means to a variety of conditions' (1979, p. 168). Gurney's position was less dogmatic than that of the early Friends because he agreed with other Christians on where they were in relation to the endtime, and only disagreed on how they had been instructed to wait.

Joint work with Anglicans in Bible Societies and later home mission work cemented this sense of British Quakerism taking its place amongst the denominations. Quakers abandoned the peculiarities of endogamy, plain dress, and plain speech in the 1850s and 1860s, although this resulted in a small conservative schism for whom this was going too far. As one British Quietist Friend said 'I would rather die as a dog in a ditch than say "you" to a single person'.

THE DISTRIBUTION

19. The 'cotton famine' created by the American Civil War caused great hardship in the Lancashire mill district in England: the Quakers ran a soup kitchen to feed Manchester's distressed, 1861

The removal of the barriers to full citizenship in Britain through the 19th century, particularly the admittance of Quakers to parliament, the professions, and the universities, gave the Quakers there a new sense of respectability and purpose. This was necessarily tinged with an occasional sense of superiority, but that should be assumed for the ongoing life of any social group. If it is not distinct and unique, why exist at all? In the late Victorian times, British Quakers modelled themselves as the 'nonconformists of the noncomformists' and 'along with Empire, the civilizing influence on the world' (Phillips, 1989, p. 53).

20th-century ecumenism

In the United States, a tripartite Quakerism (Hicksites, Gurneyites, and Wilburites) had also become 'world-accepting', abandoned the peculiarities, and increasingly worked with non-Quakers on social justice projects. Even holiness Gurneyites, such as Emma and Walter Malone, were not so wary of the world

A STEP IN REFORM.

Suggested to Mr. JOHN BRIGHT, while he is About It.

20. Cartoon suggesting John Bright, MP, extends his reforming tendencies to his dress sense and thus abandon his Quaker grey

as to not be fully involved in coordinating work in the 1890s
to alleviate the social ills of Cleveland, Ohio. The many Quakers
who were involved dressed distinctively for this work but were
not working alone. As Quakers began to organize themselves
into umbrella associations in the USA, sharing resources and
oversight, so they also became involved in ecumenism.

Friends General Conference and Five Years Meeting (now Friends
United Meeting) joined the World Council of Churches as well
as the national ecumenical bodies. North Carolina Quaker Algie
Newlin was on the first central committee of the World Council
of Churches. Evangelical Friends International are part of the
National Association of Evangelicals. Everett Cattell, leading
holiness Friend, served as President of the World Evangelical
Council.

Similarly, Quakers elsewhere in the world, such as Kenyan
Friends, joined their national Council of Churches. Quakers joined
with the other 'Historic Peace Churches', the Mennonites and The
Church of Bretheren, in dialogue and witness on peace issues, and
together they set up the New Call to Peacemaking in 1975, which
itself broadened to encompass other more ecumenical initiatives
such as 'Every Church a Peace Church'.

Internationally, Friends were involved in the World Missionary
Conference in Edinburgh in 1910 and the subsequent Jerusalem
and Madras conferences in 1928 and 1938. They were also
involved in the Faith and Order conferences in 1914, 1927, and
1937, and the Life and Work movement conferences in 1925 and
1937. (It was the collection of these conferences that led to the
proposal for the formation of the World Council of Churches in
1937.)

Within Quakerism itself, we can see the formation of the Friends
World Committee for Consultation (FWCC) in 1937 as an

ecumenical initiative. In 1920, British Friends had invited Friends from all Yearly Meetings to a conference on peace, and later in the 1920s, the American Friends Service Committee, itself a trans-yearly meeting body, set up a Fellowship Committee. This body organized a World Conference of Friends in 1937, and FWCC was established at that conference. FWCC itself has observer status at the World Council of Churches and sends representatives to meetings of Christian World Communions. Many Evangelical Yearly Meetings are not affiliated with FWCC, feeling their allegiances more closely affirmed in purely evangelical bodies, but in 1970 Everett Catell organized a conference in St Louis for all American Yearly Meetings on the theme of 'The Future of Friends', which helped further dialogue. Two international gatherings of 'Young Friends' (aged 18 to 30), in Greensboro, North Carolina, in 1986 and in Lancaster, England, in 2005, were open to Friends from all traditions and all Yearly Meetings.

Friends were full participants in the first World Parliament of Religions in Chicago in 1893. Interfaith work has grown steadily in the latter part of the 20th century. In the USA, Quakers initiated Zen Buddhist-Christian and Hindu-Christian colloquia in the 1960s and co-sponsored the Parliament of the World's Religions in 1993. In Britain, the Quaker ecumenical committee places interfaith work alongside interchurch work as part of its ecumenical work.

> Relationships beyond the Christian church embrace dialogue with other communities of faith. Individual Friends have long been active in interfaith work. Britain Yearly Meeting has not only pursued this work in the context of community relations, but has also come to appreciate the theological issues implicit in interfaith dialogue, the connections between our work for world peace, our work for understanding between faiths and the potential for mutual enrichment through interfaith sharing.
>
> (*Quaker Faith and Practice*, 1995: 9.21)

The Quaker ecumenical and interfaith committee argue that, whilst necessary and desirable, it is also more technically correct to combine interchurch and interfaith work given the root of 'ecumenical' means 'the whole people of God'. It has not been lost on this committee that even within Britain Yearly Meeting, Quakers themselves represent an ecumenical diversity. The challenge of theological diversity within an organization seeking to link with other churches is highlighted in the case study presented below, of British Quaker ecumenical relations in the 20th century.

British Quaker ecumenical relations in the 20th century

In 1986, unbidden, British Friends spent considerable time drafting a response to the World Council of Churches document, *Baptism, Eucharist, and the Ministry* (1982), published as *To Lima with Love* (1986). This process represented both a voluntary engagement with world ecumenism but also contributed to a great feeling of unity in the drafting of a response which outlined the distinctive Quaker position on authority, baptism, communion, and ministry (affirming the continuing inward and universal nature of all of these). However, over the course of the 20th century, formal membership of ecumenical bodies has been more problematic.

British Friends declined membership of the nascent WCC in 1939 and 1940 because of what many felt was its credal basis. British Friends were involved nationally ecumenically in the 1920s and 1930s, significantly in the 1939 Commission of the Churches for International Friendship and Social Responsibility. In 1942, when the British Council of Churches was formed, British Friends joined as full members under an 'exceptive clause' which allowed any church involved in the Commission to be in membership of the Council even if it could not accept its basis. In 1964, the British Council of Churches abandoned this exceptive clause as part of a constitutional review, and British Friends opted for Associate Membership.

In the 1980s, an 'Interchurch Process', of which Friends were fully a part, led to the establishment of Council of Churches for Britain and Ireland (CCBI) and four national bodies for England, Wales, Scotland, and Ireland. In 1989, British Friends agreed to apply to join the CCBI under Clause 2b, drafted to allow non-credal churches full membership. Each of the four bodies accepted London (now Britain) Yearly Meeting into membership under a clause (Clause 2b) which appears in each constitution as follows:

> A church, which on principle has no credal statements in its
> tradition and therefore cannot formally subscribe to the statement
> of faith in the Basis, may nevertheless apply for and be elected to
> full membership provided that it satisfies those member churches
> which subscribe to the Basis that it manifests faith in Christ as
> witnessed to in the Scriptures and is committed to the aims and
> purposes of the new ecumenical body, and that it will work in the
> spirit of the Basis.

The Basis reads:

> The Council of Churches for Britain and Ireland is a fellowship of
> churches in the United Kingdom of Great Britain and Northern
> Ireland and in the Republic of Ireland which confess the Lord Jesus
> Christ as God and Saviour according to the Scriptures and therefore
> seek to fulfil their common calling to the glory of the one God,
> Father, Son and Holy Spirit.

> (*Quaker Faith and Practice*, 1995: 9.09)

This membership was reaffirmed by Britain Yearly Meeting 1997.

The 1989 Yearly Meeting decision was contentious. Some felt that the distinctive approach Quakers had to Christianity was being undermined by the Basis of the new ecumenical bodies, which seemed to aspire to a doctrinal unity. For some, Clause 2b was seen to be 'merely words' and unimportant besides the spirit of cooperation. For others, the words were central and the Basis was too outward in focus. The fact that the Unitarians, who explicitly deny the Trinity, were not admitted also caused alarm as to the kind of body British Friends (who do not explicitly deny the doctrine of the Trinity but do not necessarily subscribe to it) were joining. Were the ecumenical bodies aware of the theological reality of the British Quaker group? Others felt that the permissive approach to belief, under which they had happily become part of the Yearly Meeting, was being threatened by a very public commitment to Christian ecumenism. Some were unhappy at how the application had gone ahead in spite of these misgivings. Some members resigned their membership on either side of the debate. Associate membership, had it existed in the CCBI constitution, may have satisfied the majority.

Part of the tension lay in the timing of the application to join CCBI. Quakers in Britain were during those very years involved in a delicate negotiation over how far the boundaries of acceptable belief might be extended, or what they might preclude. Some Christian Quakers were feeling excluded or anachronistic, whilst others with non-Christian theologies or ideas were also feeling unsure about where the middle ground of Quaker belief lay (see Chapter 5). In 1997, the reaffirmation of membership was far less contentious. By this stage, it was clear that the other Churches did not misunderstand the Quaker theological perspective, and also that ecumenical membership had not radically altered the ability of Friends to operate a pluralistic belief culture.

Locally, Friends have often been instrumental in setting up local councils of churches, such as the one in Bolton in 1918. Once the British Council of Churches was established, local councils tended to use the same constitution and local Quaker Meetings tended to be full members until 1964, then associate members. After

1989, some Quaker Meetings were able to negotiate covenants they could accept, others found themselves outside of their local councils.

> To sum up, meetings find themselves engaged in a variety of local ecumenical arrangements. These entail differing responsibilities and degrees of commitment to joint activity. In a time of rapid change and challenging ecumenical encounters, meetings must give careful thought to the implications of any new relationship into which they are invited to enter. They are under no obligation to enter into any formal arrangement, or to move from one kind of relationship to another. The ferment of new initiatives within and among the churches requires Friends to exercise discretion and discernment while seeking to respond to the promptings of the Spirit. We should be wary of prematurely committing our meeting; as representatives on ecumenical bodies we must be ready, on occasion, to say no even if this disappoints the expectations of the other churches. In giving effect to the concept of churches together in pilgrimage, meetings will go as far and as fast along the ecumenical road as each judges, in its local situation, to be consistent with unity in the meeting, with our understanding and practice of church government, and with Quaker testimonies and integrity.
>
> *(Quaker Faith and Practice, 1995: 9.20)*

Beyond formal membership of ecumenical bodies, there appear to be two incipient challenges for Liberal Quaker cooperation with the other Churches. The first is to do with attitudes about the Second Coming, the other regards the Liberal Quaker attitude to theology outlined in Chapter 5.

For Liberal Friends, the topic of the Second Coming is rarely spoken of. When confronted with the Second Coming message of early Friends, and the possibility that they got it wrong (in that no global transformation followed), some maintain that Friends are still in the vanguard of the Second Coming and that it is still unfolding. In other words, even whilst not talking about it, Friends are involved in some kind of slowly realizing eschatology. God's time is, after all, not the same as human time and the 'twinkling of an eye' (1 Cor. 15:52) may be taking more than 350 years. This does not ease relations with other Quakers now firmly in the meantime alongside other Christians or ecumenically. Either these Liberal Friends are the vanguard of the true Church, holding the unfolding Second Coming in trust until God wills, or else all other Christians are mistaken for believing they are still in the meantime dispensation and need to catch up, as early Friends claimed. Even where this view is held, it is done so privately and usually only offered in response to teaching about the Second Coming. Certainly, the view is not represented in any Book of Discipline.

The other challenge for Liberal Friends ecumenically is their strong belief in the necessary uncertainty of theology, described in Chapter 5 as the 'absolute perhaps'. In the same way that Quakers sometimes claim that silence is an inclusive worship method, what looks open and permissive actually is not. Holding that no group can be finally or completely or wholly right about theology presents an immediate judgement of all those religious groups who do claim even a portion of what they consider as the truth. Indeed, the Liberal Quaker position is as equally exclusive as those groups who claim their theology to be wholly true, in that they claim their view of theology to be wholly true. Of course, both the implicit views on the Second Coming and the explicit ones on the nature of theology are put aside for joint ecumenical work, as other Churches put aside their views on, for example, Quakers and the sacraments. What it means in real terms is that Liberal Quakers cannot easily subscribe to any doctrinal unity, nor even see one as intelligible. In turn, this shifts the focus of ecumenical work towards joint witness. For Evangelical Friends in the World Evangelical Alliance, the joint witness is also there but fuelled by a shared set of beliefs.

In summary, Quakers, after the first decade, increased their ecumenical and interfaith involvement over the centuries as they became more accepted and more accepting. The different Quaker traditions link to different ecumenical partnerships and have a varying commitment to intra-Quaker ecumenism. In general, theological differences are put aside where joint work on social projects can usefully be achieved.

Chapter 7
The future of Quakerism

This chapter summarizes the key areas of difference between the different traditions of Quakerism and begins to explore the future prospects of each, as well as Quakerism as a whole.

Figure 21 (pp. 108–9) lists the key points of contrast between Evangelical, Conservative, and Liberal Friends.

The first key area of difference is in terms of how Quakers define authority for belief in God. Evangelical Friends place scripture as primary, sometimes balanced by revelation. Conservative Friends place revelation as primary but find it confirmed by scripture. Liberal Friends rely on experience alone. This variation leads to a key difference in terms of how these different Quakers construct and define their Quakerism. As we saw in Chapter 4, Liberal Quakers define their Quakerism in terms of the way in which they are Quaker, that is, by what they do together as a group, the form of worship and business method, rather than in terms of doctrine. Given the primacy of experience for this group, it is the way the group achieves that experience that becomes definitional of their identity. For Evangelical Friends, their Quaker identity can be expressed largely in terms of doctrine, from which their approach to worship and their distinctive testimony flows. In Kenya, for example, formal membership is based on a two-stage doctrinal examination. For Conservative Friends, both the distinctive form of worship and the distinctive nature of Quaker-Christianity define the nature of Quakerism. What this variety means is that when different kinds of Friends meet, for example at world conferences, they are often starting from different places in how they approach the basis of their faith. For Evangelical Quakers, the Liberal tendency away from theology, their marginalization of belief and its plural nature, appears to counter the very basis of Quaker faith. For Liberals, the Evangelical tendency to see the form of worship as a pragmatic consequence of faith, rather than its core, has a similar effect.

This diversity at the very basis of how different groups construct their Quakerism is compounded by the differences in theology and in approach to theology. Evangelical Friends are Christians who happen to be Quaker. Conservative Friends are Quaker and Christian. Liberal Friends are Quakers first and foremost who may or may not be Christian or theist. Here we have a diversity of primary faith identity as well as a variation in faith content. On both counts, Quakers vary widely.

Even where theology is shared between Evangelical, Conservative, and Liberal Friends, the attitude to theology itself is not. A Christian Quaker may feel equally at home in all three traditions, depending how explicit they wish doctrine to be, and how permissive they are of theological pluralism. However, theological statements have a very different status in the three traditions, as we saw in Chapter 5. For Evangelical statements, theology can be true, accurate statements about God, who really exists. Some of this realism can be found in the Conservative tradition, although some Conservatives also understand theology as symbolic. In the Liberal tradition, what is experienced (God or 'God' or not-God-but) is real, but the statements used to describe that experience cannot be wholly or completely accurate. Except in very general terms, theological statements are a personal

Evangelical	Conservative	Liberal
Scripture and spiritual experience as primary	Spiritual experience as primary, scripture as secondary	Experience as primary
Defined by belief	Defined by belief and form	Defined in terms of method/form
Christian identity primary	'Quaker' identity primary	'Quaker' identity primary
Christian	Christ-centred	Christian, post-Christian, and non-theist
Realism	Realism and semi-realism	Semi-realism and non-realism
Final and complete and whole Truth possible. Theology as True, not just story.	Final and complete and whole Truth possible. Theology as True, not just story.	Truth only personal, partial, or provisional. Theology always a 'towards' kind of activity. The 'absolute perhaps'.

Programmed or semi-programmed worship	Unprogrammed worship	Unprogrammed worship
Pastors – visible and active	No visible leadership	No visible leadership
Restraint of emotion variable church by church	Restraint of emotion	Restraint of emotion
Mission Christianity seen as salvific	Limited outreach Quakerism as salvific	Outreach Quakerism seen as optional
Traditional teaching on sexual morality	Mix of traditional and liberal teaching on sexual morality	Politically liberal on sexual morality
Inclusive	Exclusive?	Exclusive?

21. Areas of difference between Evangelical, Conservative, and Liberal Friends

interpretation. (Non-theists are the exception to this position because they claim to *know* that there is no God. In other words, their claim that God is a fiction is seen as a wholly accurate theological statement. In this they are paradoxically 'realist' about their non-realism.) For Liberals, then, theological statements tend to be personal, partial, or provisional only in terms of truth claims, and theology as a whole is a 'perhaps' kind of activity, an attempt to get forever closer to something which ultimately cannot be fully known or described. From Chapter 5, Liberal Friends operate a 'doctrine' of absolute (rationally certain) 'perhapsness' about theology. For Evangelicals and Conservatives, theological statements need not be perhaps and can represent truth for all people for all time.

There are differences in worship too. As we saw in Chapter 3, a theology of direct encounter and divine guidance still informs the majority of all three traditions. It is simply that worship is organized in different ways. In the Evangelical tradition, pastors seek God's guidance to help plan the worship and follow the leading of the Holy Spirit during the worship event. At some stage during worship, there is the opportunity in most Friends' Churches for everyone to experience inward communion, and in those places it is seen to be the focus of the worship, what all else leads to and helps prepare the Meeting for. Semi-programmed Meetings have extended periods of both programmed elements and 'open worship'. In the Conservative and Liberal traditions, there are no pastors and there is no pre-programming of worship other than the regular pattern of silent worship. Elders may contribute in spoken or unspoken ways but, in other words, these two latter traditions focus entirely on the experience of encounter and communion, rather than using programmed elements to help people prepare for it. This open and minimalist form needs little explicit leadership and where there are paid staff in these traditions, they often work centrally, helping provide resources for all the Meetings, rather than locally. Where Meetings have a pastor, the style of worship is finalized locally and may change in tone and content with different leadership styles as pastors change. One variation in this regard is the level of outward expression and emotion encouraged by the pastor, for example through the choice of music. In the Conservative and Liberal traditions, displays of extreme emotion are rare. Silence is the corporate activity, expression an individual one. It is largely an auditory form of worship, rather than a visual or physical one.

Mission work is critical to the Evangelical faith. Salvation is potentially universal, and Christ's love for humanity demands Christians respond in trying to share the faith more widely. The Great Commission (Matthew 28:16–20) is explicit about this. For Conservative Friends, salvation is mentioned less, but is still a key part of the faith and is also seen as universal. However, as with all Friends, they have abandoned the claim to represent the sole true Church, and mission or 'outreach' is limited. Liberal Friends talk very little of salvation and have a different view on the purposes of religion, some seeing it as helpful rather than essential: not only may others find other Churches where they are more at home, but other faiths or no faith. Outreach is conducted as information, the presentation of the Quaker option, but is very low key, and no attempts to proselytize are made.

In the same way that there is no necessary link between Evangelical faith and programmed worship and Liberal faith and unprogrammed worship, there is also no necessary link between Evangelicalism *per se* and political conservatism (save where scripture is read literally) and Liberal Quakerism and political liberalism, but the traditions do tend to polarize in this way. This is especially true of questions of sexual morality, although Evangelicals are themselves divided over issues such as homosexuality and abortion. Conservatives vary widely in their political views but tend to uphold the sanctity of marriage and monogamous commitment, whereas Liberals have a more plural approach to sexual morality. The focus in the Liberal tradition is on the fruits of the relationship, rather than its form. Liberals hold no one view on abortion or on homosexuality, but many lesbians and gays have found a welcoming spiritual home within the Liberal tradition. In other areas of lifestyle, Friends would find more common ground across the traditions, wishing to simplify consumption, maintain integrity, and show regard for the environment.

Evangelical Quakerism is ultimately more inclusive. It both seeks and welcomes everyone, even when that inclusivity has meant leaving behind aspects of Quaker tradition. Conservative and Liberal Quakerism, with Quaker identity as primary, tends to be more exclusive, welcoming those for whom Quakerism is the right path, but placing little effort on mission. These two traditions have each maintained, albeit in very different ways, a faith they present as distinctively Quaker. They use traditional Quaker terms and worship in a way that is very different from other Churches.

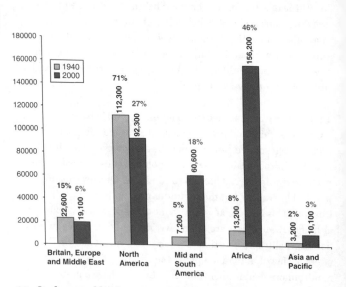

22. Quakers worldwide, 1940 and 2000

They are more sectarian, as opposed to the more denominational approach taken by the Evangelical tradition. This different emphasis towards mission and exclusivity is most evident if we look at the change in the composition of world Quakerism between 1940 and 2000.

In 1940, there were 157,800 Friends worldwide. In 2000, this figure had risen to 338,000. Figure 22 shows that the major changes in numerical strength are in Mid and South America and in Africa, the new strongholds of Evangelical Quakerism. Taken together, the increases there account for the worldwide increase, also offsetting some losses in North America and Europe. As mission work continues, now from within these indigenous Yearly Meetings, we can expect these numbers to continue to grow. These figures also denote a major shift in the geographical location of the majority of Friends, as well as a shift, in percentage terms, towards programmed Quakerism representing the vast majority of Friends. In 2000, 83% of Friends were in Yearly Meetings where the worship is programmed; only 9% of Friends belonged to wholly unprogrammed Yearly Meetings; 8% to those affiliated to both Liberal and Evangelical umbrella groups (FGC and FUM). Liberal Quaker numbers are falling worldwide. In Britain, for example, there are 472 Meetings, but numbers in formal membership have dropped from the 20th-century high of about 22,000 in 1958 to about 15,000 in 2006.

In 1940, North American Friends represented 71% of world Quakerism; in 2000 the figure was 27%. North America and Europe together represent only one-third of world Quakerism, a significant development given the way the tradition has been transmitted from those Yearly Meetings and the status which in the past has been accorded older Yearly Meetings. Still today, the bulk of Quaker staff and plant resources, and the bulk of Quaker publishing, is located in North America and Europe and is in English. More Quaker publications are being translated into Spanish, but we can see that at present rates of growth, majority Quakerism will soon be African, and in particular Kenyan – of the 156,000 Friends in Africa, over 133,000 are in Kenya.

Evangelical Quaker missionaries travel worldwide and have been instrumental in establishing Friends' churches even within heartlands of unprogrammed Quakerism such as Philadelphia. Should their attention turn to the renewal of Quakerism rather than the promotion of Christianity, we could expect African Quaker missionaries to travel to other parts of the Quaker world, once the resources are available. Certainly, world Quaker leadership is likely to come in increasing numbers from Africa and Mid and South America. What that in turn may bring are further negotiations over what constitutes authentic Quakerism, as newer Yearly Meetings, and those furthest away from the traditional centres of Quakerism (London and Philadelphia) have, historically, tended to innovate the most. The resource gap remains huge at present, as does, potentially, the willingness of white Quakers to learn from black Friends, particularly those of a different worship tradition.

This may mean that Liberal and Conservative Quaker groups, already low in numbers, may become sectarian remnants, reluctant to be allied to the majority of 'the world family of Friends', and possibly even each other, given their theological differences. The Conservative Quaker world has recently extended itself through the provision by Ohio Yearly Meeting of associate membership for those who feel spiritually isolated (often within more Liberal Yearly Meetings), and Ohio now has members in Europe and elsewhere. North Carolina Conservative has become more Liberal in recent years as it covers land where the Conservative Meetings represent the only unprogrammed option. As such, they have attracted Liberal Quakers moving into the area. However, it is still clearly in the Conservative tradition.

If Liberal Friends continue to diversify theologically and/or continue to move away from a Christian base, their connection with the Quaker tradition would be purely in terms of their worship method, witness, historical association, and name. With many of those coming into membership seeing themselves as 'refugees' from organized Christianity, and half coming from no immediately prior religious affiliation, the inclination to be part of a mainly Evangelical world Quaker family is low. Moreover, if the reference point for the group moves from the transcendent to the subjective, this form of Quakerism would come to represent an option within what Heelas and Woodhead have termed the 'holistic milieu', rather than the religious world. In other words, this form of Quakerism would become increasingly focused on the subjective. This would be in accord with much of European religiosity and could stem the falling numbers. But evidence also shows that those attracted to this form of person-centred spirituality are less inclined to join in with organized groups. And in terms of adherence to form, and the jargon used to describe it, Liberal Quakers still look like a sect.

However, there are also signs of religious renewal amongst Liberal Friends. Writers like Benjamin Lloyd (2007) and initiatives such as 'Quaker Quest' (a rolling programme of public talks on Quakerism initiated in London) represent a clarity over the strengths of Liberal Quakerism and a refusal to 'dumb down' descriptions of its spiritual core. Some of the analysis of the diversification of belief within Liberal Quakerism, as we saw in Chapter 5, was around the invisibility of belief, and the anxiety such invisibility gave those wishing to share more. These kinds of new currents represent a solidly theist approach unafraid to say so, and this may both create a clear 'line in the sand' as to how far Liberal Quakerism can mutate, as well as offering those inside the group, and those coming in, a clear sense of what is central theologically. Diffuse beliefs and belief transmission have been seen to make liberal religious associations particularly vulnerable, but these trends counter both of these danger-points, and may help bring in those happy to worship in silence and to seek within a theist framework without being too theologically explicit. As for those who predicted the end of cinema-going in the 1960s, so the graphs of terminal decline (for example, showing Friends in Britain will have disappeared by 2032) may prove to be over-deterministic.

For Evangelical Friends, the tension is over the degree to which they maintain a distinctive Quaker approach or adopt a more mainstream liturgical formula and witness, and become community churches, or quasi-mainline. Yorba Linda Friends' Church, California, one of the fastest-growing Friends' Churches, involves over 3,500 in worship each weekend and runs buses to the church from nearby shopping malls. However, the term 'Quaker' is less prevalent than it used to be, and baptism is offered quarterly. Partly, this is because of its association with Liberal Friends, but also because in the religious shopfront, 'Quaker' conjures up sectarian peculiarity, silence rather than vibrance. As mentioned above, some of these churches now permit water baptism or practise occasional outward communion. These may in themselves undermine some of the core and shared Quaker understandings, for example about the inward encounter. The bigger and perhaps more telling tensions may be those over aspects of Quaker testimony, in particular testimony against war. Where this, as well as inward communion, disappears from the collective Friends' Church understanding, then nothing stands in the way of these groups becoming mainstream Protestant Churches. In the USA, Evangelical numbers are not rising, and these sectarian/denominational tensions are highly contested in terms of how this form of Quakerism should present itself.

Beyond the individual church, Evangelical Friends are divided over the questions of abortion and, in particular, homosexuality.

The desire of some Friends' churches to recognize homosexuals as members or to permit 'celebrations of commitment' for same-sex couples has led to schism and secession. This debate of course increases the perceived distance between Evangelical and Liberal Friends.

Quakerism as a whole is numerically healthy and growing. If present rates continue, African Quakerism will represent the vast majority of Friends worldwide in the next 50 years, whilst secularization in Europe and North America will have depleted particularly the Liberal tendency there, depending on how far it can adapt to its new areligious context. At present, the key fourfold common ground of the world family of Friends remains intact and comprises:

23. A young Quaker protester at the inauguration of George W. Bush with 'War is not the Answer' sign, sponsored by the Friends Committee on National Legislation (FCNL), 20 January 2005

1) the centrality of direct inward encounter with God and revelation, and, thus, forms of worship that allow this to be experienced;

2) a way of doing church business based on the idea of corporate direct guidance rather than voting;

3) the spiritual equality of everyone, and the idea of 'the priesthood of all believers';

4) based in part on the latter, the preference for peace and pacifism rather than war, and the commitment to other forms of social witness.

Witness, rooted in that experience of the direct encounter and the belief in spiritual equality and universal salvation, continues. Peace witness in particular continues worldwide in the name of Friends, and Quakers remain, through their liturgical form, and their witness work, a distinctive group still working for the Kingdom that its founders felt so near at hand.

References

Robert Barclay, *Apology for the True Christian Divinity* (Glenside, Pennsylvania: Quaker Heritage Press, 2002 [1678]).

Richard Bauman, *Let Your Words Be Few: Symbolism of Speaking and Silence amongst Seventeenth-Century Quakers* (Cambridge: Cambridge University Press, 1983).

David Boulton, *The Trouble with God: Religious Humanism and the Republic of Heaven* (Hampshire: John Hunt Publishing, 2002).

William C. Braithwaite, *The Beginnings of Quakerism* (London: Macmillan, 1912).

Edward Burrough, *A Trumpet Sounded Forth Out of Sion* (London: Giles Calvert, 1656).

Kathryn Damiano, 'On Earth as it is in Heaven: Eighteenth-Century Quakerism as Realized Eschatology', unpublished PhD thesis, Union of Experimenting Colleges and Universities, 1988.

Richard S. Dunn and Mary M. Dunn (eds), *The Papers of William Penn, Volume Two, 1680–1684* (Philadelphia, PA: University of Pennsylvania Press, 1982).

Faith and Practice – Book of Discipline of the North Carolina Yearly Meeting (Conservative) of the Religious Society of Friends (NC, 1983).

Faith and Practice, North Pacific Yearly Meeting of the Religious Society of Friends (Corvallis, OR, 1993).

Faith and Practice of Evangelical Friends Church Southwest (Whittier, CA, 2001).

Faith and Practice: A Book of Christian Discipline, Northwest Yearly Meeting of Friends Church (Newberg, OR, 2003).

Margaret Fell, *A Brief Collection of Remarkable Passages and Occurrences Relating to Margaret Fell* (London: J. Sowle, 1710).

George Fox, *Works*, vol. 8 (State College, Pennsylvania: New Foundation Publications, 1990).

Joseph J. Gurney, *A Peculiar People: The Rediscovery of Primitive Christianity* (Richmond, Indiana: Friends United Press, 1979; transcript of *Observations on the Distinguishing Views and Practices of the Society of Friends*, seventh edn, 1834).

Douglas Gwyn, *Covenant Crucified: Quakers and the Rise of Capitalism* (Wallingford, Pennsylvania: Pendle Hill, 1995).

Thomas D. Hamm, *The Transformation of American Quakerism: Orthodox Friends 1800–1907* (Bloomington: Indiana University Press, 1988).

Jonathan Hewitt (1990), 'Embracing Uncertainty', *The Friend* (1990), 148, pp. 757–8.

Rufus M. Jones, *The Later Periods of Quakerism*, 2 vols (London: Macmillan, 1921).

Daniel Leichty, *Theology in Postliberal Perspective* (London: SCM, 1990).

Benjamin Lloyd, *Turnaround: Growing a Twenty-First Century Religious Society of Friends*, Pendle Hill Pamphlet 387 (Wallingford, Pennsylvania: Pendle Hill, 2007).

Charles Mylander (ed.), *Welcome to Friends* (Whittier, CA: Evangelical Friends Church Southwest, 2004).

John Nickalls, *The Journal of George Fox* (Cambridge: Cambridge University Press, 1952).

Brian D. Phillips, 'Friendly Patriotism: British Quakerism and the Imperial Nation, 1890–1910', unpublished PhD thesis, University of Cambridge, 1989.

John Punshon, *Letter to a Universalist*, Pendle Hill Pamphlet 285 (Wallingford, Pennsylvania: Pendle Hill, 1989).

Quaker Faith and Practice: The Book of Christian Discipline in the Yearly Meeting of the Religious Society of Friends (Quakers) in Britain (London: Britain Yearly Meeting, 1995).

Barry Reay, *The Quakers and the English Revolution* (London: Temple Smith, 1985).

The Quaker Way (London: Quaker Home Service, 1998).

To Lima with Love. Baptism, Eucharist and Ministry: A Quaker Response (London: Quaker Home Service, 1986).

Dorothy White, *Friends, you that are of the Parliament, hear the word of the Lord* (1659).

Dorothy White, *A Call from God out of Egypt* (1662).

Further reading

In Britain, the main libraries are at Friends House, London, and at Woodbrooke Quaker Study Centre, Birmingham. In the USA, there are notable historical collections at Swarthmore College and Haverford College, just outside of Philadelphia, and at Earlham College, Richmond, Indiana, and Guilford College, Greensboro, North Carolina. George Fox University in Newberg, Oregon, also has a Quaker collection.

The main Quaker booksellers are the Quaker Bookshop, Friends House in London, Pendle Hill Bookstore in Wallingford, Pennsylvania, Friends General Conference Quaker Books in Philadelphia, and Friends United Meeting Bookstore, Richmond, Indiana. These all supply mail order with online catalogues.

The two main journals in the USA are *Friends Journal* and *Quaker Life*. In Britain, the independent Quaker journal, *The Friend*, is published weekly.

For general reading, look out for leaflets in Meeting Houses. For insight into Year Meeting belief and practice, get hold of the local 'Book of Discipline' or 'Faith and Practice'. These are written for Quakers and may include 'insider' jargon and possibly more administrative detail than is helpful to the newcomer, but should also give a definite flavour of that Yearly Meeting's Quaker faith.

The best paperback introductions to Quaker history and thought are: Marge Abbott et al., *The A–Z of the Friends (Quakers)* (Scarecrow Press, 2006); Michael Birkel, *Silence and Witness* (Orbis Books, 2004); Will Cooper, *A Living Faith: An Historical and Comparative Study of Quaker Beliefs* (Friends United Press, 2001); Pink Dandelion, *Introduction to Quakerism* (Cambridge University Press, 2007); John Punshon *Portrait in Grey: A Short History of the Quakers* (Quaker Books, 2006); and Walter Williams *The Rich Heritage of Quakerism* (Barclay Press, 1989). Thomas D. Hamm's *Quakerism in America* (Columbia University Press, 2003) provides a detailed discussion of the three streams of contemporary Quakerism in North America.

The best books on the early Friends still in print are: Hugh Barbour and Arthur Roberts, *Early Quaker Writings 1650–1700* (Pendle Hill, 2004); Richard Bauman, *Let Your Words Be Few* (Quaker Home Service, 1998); Douglas Gwyn's trilogy, *Apocalypse of the Word: The Life and Message of George Fox, 1624–1691* (Friends United Press, 1986), *Covenant Crucified: Quakers and the Rise of Capitalism* (Quaker Books, 2006), and *Seekers Found: Atonement in Early Quaker Experience* (Pendle Hill, 1995); and Rosemary Moore, *The Light in Their Consciences: The Early Quakers in Britain 1646–1666* (Pennsylvania State University Press, 2000).

Fox's complete works are available in eight volumes (New Foundation Publications, 1990). His journal is most widely available in the versions edited by John Nickalls (Philadelphia Yearly Meeting, 1997) and Nigel Smith (Penguin, 1998). William Penn's *No Cross, No Crown* is reprinted by Sessions of York, and Barclay's *Apology* in its first edition has been republished by Quaker Heritage Press in 2002. Quaker Heritage Press also carry many early Quaker texts online, as does the Digital Quaker Collection at Earlham College.

The Braithwaite/Jones Rowntree Quaker History series, published in seven volumes after 1911 is excellent but is now out of print. William Braithwaite's *The Beginnings of Quakerism* and *The Second Period of Quakerism* offer the most comprehensive overview available of early Quaker history. Facsimile editions published by Sessions in 1980 are still available in some Quaker bookshops.

Other excellent histories in print include: Thomas Hamm, *The Transformation of American Quakerism: Orthodox Friends 1800-1907* (Indiana University Press, 1988) and Thomas Kennedy, *British Quakerism 1860-1920: The Transformation of a Religious Community* (Oxford University Press, 2001).

Overviews of the history of Quaker theology include: Pink Dandelion, *The Liturgies of Quakerism* (Ashgate, 2005) and Carole Spencer, *Holiness: The Soul of Quakerism* (Paternoster, 2007).

Biographical works on leading Friends include: Margaret Hope Bacon, *Valiant Friend: The Life of Lucretia Mott* (Friends General Conference, 1999); Leo Damrosch, *The Sorrows of the Quaker Jesus: James Nayler and the Puritan Crackdown on the Free Spirit* (Harvard University Press, 1996); Elsa Glines (ed.), *Undaunted Zeal: The Letters of Margaret Fell* (Friends United Press, 2003); Mike Heller (ed.), *The Tendering Presence: Essays on John Woolman* (Pendle Hill, 2003); H. Larry Ingle, *First Among Friends: George Fox and the Creation of Quakerism* (Oxford University Press, 1994); Gil Skidmore, *Elizabeth Fry – A Quaker Life: Selected Writings and Letters* (Altamira, 2005).

Timeline

1534	Henry VIII breaks with Rome.
1611	King James I Authorized Version of the Bible widely distributed.
1624	Birth of George Fox.
1642	Beginning of the English Civil War.
1647	George Fox has the opening that 'there is one, even Christ Jesus, that can speak to thy condition'.
1649	Execution of King Charles I; Oliver Cromwell and the Puritans govern in England.
1652	George Fox's vision on Pendle Hill of a great people to be gathered.
1654	'Valiant Sixty' missionary work.
1656	James Nayler's entry into Bristol and trial by Parliament.
1656	First Friends arrive in North America. Others set off for the Vatican and the Sultan of Constantinople.
1658	Death of Oliver Cromwell.
1659–61	Four Quakers hanged, on Boston Common; anti-Quaker laws enacted in Virginia.
1660	Death of James Nayler. Restoration of King Charles II.
1661	First General Meeting held in Newport, Rhode Island, start of New England Yearly Meeting, the oldest such body in the world.

	Publication in England of *A Declaration from the Harmless and Innocent People of God, called Quakers*, first public statement of the testimony against outward war.
1662	'Quaker Acts' forbid Quakers to meet in England.
1668	First Quaker schools in England. London Yearly Meeting established.
1676	Robert Barclay's *Apology* published; Meeting for Sufferings organized in London.
1681	William Penn obtains charter for Pennsylvania; Philadelphia Yearly Meeting established.
1683	First Friends' school in North America.
1688	Germantown Meeting in Pennsylvania protests against slavery.
1689	Toleration Act in England passed. Death of Robert Barclay.
1691	Death of George Fox.
1694	Publication of George Fox's *Journal*.
1702	Death of Margaret Fell
1722	Recording of Ministers established in Britain.
1737	Lists of Settlement create a formal list of members.
1756	Quakers relinquish control of Pennsylvania legislature.
1758	Philadelphia Yearly Meeting condemns slaveholding by Friends.
1783	First 'Book of Extracts' (Book of Discipline) published in Britain.
1796	York Retreat, the first modern mental hospital, is founded by Friends in Britain.
1808	John Dalton states atomic theory.
1813	Elizabeth Fry begins prison reform work at Newgate Prison in England.
1817	Friends Asylum, the first modern mental hospital in the US, founded in Frankford, Pennsylvania.
1825	Edward Pease opens the Stockton and Darlington Railway, the first passenger railway in England.
1827–8	The Great Separation in North America into Hicksite and Orthodox branches.

1833	Joseph Pease elected to the British Parliament; John Greenleaf Whittier published.
1837	Joseph John Gurney travels to America.
1843	John Bright enters British Parliament. Indiana Yearly Meeting of Anti-Slavery Friends separates from Indiana Yearly Meeting.
1845	The Gurneyite-Wilburite separation in New England.
1846	Levi Coffin settles in Cincinnati, Ohio, and becomes known as 'president' of the 'underground railroad'.
1846–7	Quaker famine relief in Ireland.
1847	Adult School and Home Mission movements in Britain become established.
1848	Lucretia Mott initiates organization of the first women's rights convention in Seneca Falls, New York.
1852	Friends Temperance Union formed in Britain.
1854	Gurneyite-Wilburite separation in Ohio.
1859	Endogamy discontinued in Britain.
1860	Conference held at Ackworth, England, for active consideration of new forms of foreign missionary work by Friends.
1862	American Quakers undertake relief and educational work for freed slaves.
1866	Rachel Metcalf sent by British Friends to undertake missionary work in India; American Friends undertake supervision of Indian agencies in Nebraska, Kansas, and Indian Territories; Sybil and Eli Jones sent by New York Yearly Meeting as missionaries to Ramallah, Palestine, and help establish school for girls there.
c. 1875	Introduction of 'pastoral system' among American Friends.
1887	Richmond Declaration of Faith adopted by most Gurneyite North American Yearly Meetings.
1895	Manchester Conference held in England, with Summer Schools held in subsequent years, culminating in opening of Woodbrooke Quaker Study Centre in 1903.
1900	Friends General Conference (FGC) established.

Timeline

1902	Five Years Meeting (FYM, renamed Friends United Meeting (FUM) in 1965) established.
1903	Willis R. Hotchkiss, Arthur B. Chilson, and Edgar Hole sent by FYM to East Africa.
1909	First fully united men's and women's London Yearly Meeting.
1914	War Victim's Relief Committee established by British Friends. Friends Ambulance Unit created to provide care for soldiers and civilians injured in World War I.
1917	American Friends Service Committee (AFSC) established.
1919–24	Friends undertake feeding programme for German children; programme then expands into Poland, Russia, and other European countries.
1937	Friends World Committee for Consultation established.
1937–9	Non-partisan relief work in Spanish Civil War.
1939–46	Quaker war relief in Europe and Asia.
1940	Civilian Public Service camps for conscientious objectors to war established by US government and administered by AFSC.
1945	New England Yearly Meetings reunite.
1947	Nobel Peace Prize awarded to AFSC and Friends Service Council (Britain) on behalf of the Religious Society of Friends.
1946	East Africa Yearly Meeting formed, the first such body in Africa.
1955	Meetings divided by 1827 separation rejoin, forming united Yearly Meetings in New York, Canada, and Philadelphia.
1963–4	Establishment of Evangelical Friends Alliance (becoming Evangelical Friends International (EFI) in 1990).
1967	Separated Yearly Meetings in the Middle Atlantic states form the consolidated Baltimore Yearly Meeting.
1999	EFI-Africa Region open the Great Lakes School of Theology at Bujumbura, Burundi.

The Quakers

Glossary

apostasy: The state of falling away from the faith, used in particular by early Quakers as a criticism of other Christians.

Beaconites: The name given to the followers of Isaac Crewdson who separated from Meetings in the London Yearly Meeting (particularly Manchester and Kendal) in 1836. Crewdson had referred to the idea of the 'Inward Light' as delusional in his publication *A Beacon to the Society of Friends* published in 1835, and in general offered what has since been termed an 'ultra-evangelical' critique of British Quakerism.

Book of Discipline: An anthology of useful extracts from previous *minutes* or Quaker writings compiled to guide and nurture Quakers and their Meetings in their discipleship. Each *Yearly Meeting* has its own Book of Discipline and they are regularly revised.

Business Meeting: A meeting for worship concerned with decisions to do with the life of the Meeting, such as finance or property. No votes are taken, but the *Clerk* prepares a *minute* reflecting 'the sense of the Meeting' which is agreed in the Meeting. Unity is seen as a sign of discerning God's will accurately, disunity as a sign that further work needs to be done, perhaps at a later date.

centring down: The process by which individual Quakers deepen their worship experience.

Clerks: Those who guide the process of Quaker *Business Meetings*. They also typically handle the correspondence of the Meeting.

concern: A 'leading' from God to action. Quakers talk of having a 'concern laid on them'.

Conservative Quakers: The tradition of Quakerism which attempts to conserve Quaker faith and practice. As such, it uses the more traditional 'unprogrammed' form of worship whilst remaining Christ-centred in its theology.

convincement: Whilst technically meaning 'conviction', one of the elements of the transformation experienced by early Friends, the term is used more popularly to refer to the whole of the transformation experience. Today it can also be used less specifically to refer to those who have come into membership as adults, 'by convincement'.

deism: The theological idea that God, having created the world, like a clock-maker, left creation to its own devices. This places responsibility directly into humanity's hands and tends to support a rationalist approach to theology and faith.

discernment: The process by which Quakers decide what is truly from God.

disownment: The process by which Quakers lose their formal membership. This is a Meeting decision and is typically based on major misdemeanour or misrepresentation of Quakerism. The practice was very prevalent in the 18th century, particularly for 'marrying out' (that is, marrying a non-Quaker), but is rare today.

Elders: Those appointed to nurture the *ministry* of the members and the *Meeting for Worship*. Elders can be associated with the disciplining of the Meeting, and Friends talk of having been 'eldered' when reminded of Quaker practice.

endogamy: The practice of marrying only those within your group.

endtime: The phrase used to refer to the end of the world, as foretold in the Book of Revelation, and the realization for the elect of the Kingdom of Heaven.

eschatology: The term used to refer to theological ideas about the *endtime*. Eschatological means 'to do with endtime theology'.

Evangelical Friends: Evangelicalism is a form of Christianity focused on scriptural authority, the spreading of the Gospel through mission, and salvation, made possible through Christ's atoning death on the cross. These ideas inform the Evangelical tradition of Quakerism, which emerged at the end of the 18th century and which today represents over 80% of all Quakers worldwide.

familied monasticism: The term used to describe the preference amongst 18th-century Quakers for a guarded home life which was designed to protect Quakers from the corrupt and corrupting nature of the wider *world*.

General Meeting: A regional gathering, midway in size between a *Monthly* and *Yearly Meeting*. In Britain, General Meetings used to be called *Quarterly Meetings*.

Great Separation: The division between *Hicksite* and *Orthodox* Friends in 1827, beginning in the Philadelphia Yearly Meeting but spreading to most other US Yearly Meetings. The dispute was partly over the authority given the Inward Light as opposed to scripture.

Gurneyite: The term given to those *Orthodox* Friends who followed the teachings of *Evangelical* Quaker Joseph John Gurney in opposition to those who followed John Wilbur, thus causing a further round of schisms within Orthodox Quakerism in the 1840s and 1850s.

Hicksite: The name given to the followers of Elias Hicks, who separated from *Orthodox* Friends as part of the *Great Separation* of 1827. They tended to emphasize Quaker practice and the authority of the Inward Light.

higher criticism: Scholarship concerned with calculating how the Bible was put together and by whom it was written.

holiness: A mystical expression of Christianity which comprises a sense of being transformed and set apart for God's purposes. It was very prevalent amongst those Friends influenced by the interdenominational *Revivalist* movement of the 1860s onwards and is still dominant in some *Evangelical* Quaker Meetings.

leading: A sense of being directed by God in a particular direction. Quakers talk of 'having leadings'.

Liberal Quakers: Based on a rationalist expression of Christianity, one of the three main Quaker traditions in the modern world. Beginning in the late 19th century, it is characterized today by a permissive attitude to belief and caution over explicit theology.

meantime: The term used to refer to the time in which humanity waits for the *endtime*.

Meeting for Sufferings: Originally set up to petition government on behalf of Friends suffering in prison, these became powerful interim committees of their *Yearly Meetings*. In Britain, Meeting for Sufferings is concerned with major policy decisions. It is comprised of representatives from each *Monthly Meeting*.

Meeting for Worship: The term used to refer to Quaker worship, rather than 'service'. Quakers talk of 'going to meeting' rather than going to church.

meeting house: The name given to the places built intentionally to house Quaker worship.

minister: Those believed to have a 'gift' of *ministry*. In some *Yearly Meetings*, this term is used for those who are specifically 'recorded' by the *Monthly Meetings* as having the gift of ministry.

ministry: In its broadest sense, the term used to describe the particular calling given to everyone by God. For example, somebody may be described as having a 'ministry of hospitality'. Also and more commonly used to refer to vocal ministry given in *Meeting for Worship*.

minutes: Quakers have proved to be assiduous record-keepers over time, one principal source being the minutes of all their Meetings. These are always agreed by the whole Meeting (be it Monthly or Yearly) within the Meeting.

modernist: A sociological term used to describe a cultural movement founded on rationalist thought, as opposed to romantic or theological ideals. Marked by the love of what is modern and contemporary, and in general by differentiation between categories, such as science and faith.

Monthly Meeting: The body of Friends which holds responsibility for membership and property, and also the name of the monthly *Business Meeting* to discuss these and other matters. A Monthly Meeting is usually part of a *Yearly Meeting*. It may have its own constituent *Preparative Meetings*.

Nominations Committee: The committee which '*discerns*' whose name should be suggested to a *Business Meeting* for appointment to a particular role, such as *Clerk* or *Elder*.

non-realism: Within theology, the philosophical idea that God does not exist and as such that theological statements cannot be true.

Orthodox: The name given to the *Evangelical Friends* who broke away from the *Hicksites* in the *Great Separation* of 1827. They tended to define Quakerism in terms of belief and emphasized scriptural authority.

Overseer: The name traditionally given to those who are concerned with the pastoral needs of the Meeting.

peculiarities: The collective term for the numerous ways Friends traditionally separated themselves from 'the *world*', such as *plain speech and dress*, the numbering of days and months instead of naming them.

plain dress: The term used to describe the way in which Friends dressed in uniform and simple manner, distinctive in its grey or black colour and unadorned style from worldly fashions. This practice began with the first Friends and lasted until the 20th century. A very few Friends still adopt plain dress.

plain speech: The refusal to use the polite form 'you' to social superiors but to use 'thee' and 'thou' to everyone. The term also refers to the way in which Quakers attempted to cut any superfluity such as small talk from their conversation.

Preparative Meeting: A constituent meeting of a *Monthly Meeting*, usually holding its own monthly *Business Meeting* in preparation for the Monthly Meeting. In Britain, local Meetings are called Preparative Meetings but in America the local Meeting is called a Monthly Meeting, with only a *Quarterly* or *General Meetings* between themselves and the *Yearly Meeting*.

progressivism: The doctrine maintaining humanity necessarily learns more about the nature of God over time. Future generations will know more than the present one.

Quarterly Meeting: A regional meeting for business comprising several *Monthly Meetings* which meets quarterly.

Quietist Quakers: The name given to 18th-century Friends influenced by the self-denying mysticism of the continental Quietists such as Guyon, Fenelon, and Molinos. They emphasized the inward nature of true spirituality and a desire for humility and obedience.

realism: Within theology, the philosophical idea that God exists and that theological statements can be true and accurate.

Renewal: One of the competing branches of *Gurneyite* Quakerism in the 1870s (the other was *Revival* Quakerism), Renewal Friends wanted to modernize Quakerism and work more with others on social justice projects, whilst retaining a distinctive practice.

Revival: One of the competing branches of *Gurneyite* Quakerism in the 1870s (the other was *Renewal* Quakerism), Revival Friends placed *holiness* at the centre of their faith and tended to be wary of the *world* whilst open to other holiness Christians.

semi-realism: Within theology, the philosophical idea that whilst God exists, statements about God necessarily fall short in their attempt to match words to experience and cannot be considered to be objectively accurate.

travelling in the ministry: The term used to describe the way in which Friends travel 'under *concern*' to other parts of the Quaker and wider *world* to share their *ministry*. This is typically supported with a *minute* from the Friends' home Meetings.

Wilburite: The name given to followers of John Wilbur, who separated from *Gurneyite* Friends in the 1840s and 1850s, in particular over how far scriptural authority was greater than that of revelation; Wilburites favoured a balance of both.

world: The pejorative term used by the first Quakers to describe anything not Quaker. Over time, what constitutes 'the world' has shrunk; what Quakers consider 'too worldly' varies between traditions.

Yearly Meeting: The term used to describe an independent body of Friends comprised of various *Monthly Meetings*, as well as the annual gathering of those Friends. Thus, someone can both be a part of a Yearly Meeting and attend sessions that meet up yearly. They vary widely in size, from about 30 members in, say, Denmark Yearly Meeting, to 22,000 in one of the Bolivian Yearly Meetings. Some Yearly Meetings hold a half-year's meeting as well.

Index

Visit the
VERY SHORT
INTRODUCTIONS
Web site

www.oup.co.uk/vsi

➤ **Information** about all published titles

➤ News of **forthcoming books**

➤ **Extracts** from the books, including titles not yet published

➤ **Reviews** and views

➤ **Links** to other **web sites** and main OUP web page

➤ Information about **VSIs in translation**

➤ **Contact** the editors

➤ **Order** other **VSIs** on-line

Expand your collection of
VERY SHORT INTRODUCTIONS

THEOLOGY
A Very Short Introduction
David F. Ford

This Very Short Introduction provides both believers and non-believers with a balanced survey of the central questions of contemporary theology. David Ford's interrogative approach draws the reader into considering the principles underlying religious belief, including the centrality of salvation to most major religions, the concept of God in ancient, modern, and post-modern contexts, the challenge posed to theology by prayer and worship, and the issue of sin and evil. He also probes the nature of experience, knowledge, and wisdom in theology, and discusses what is involved in interpreting theological texts today.

'David Ford tempts his readers into the huge resources of theology with an attractive mix of simple questions and profound reflection. With its vivid untechnical language it succeeds brilliantly in its task of introduction.'

Stephen Sykes, University of Durham

'a fine book, imaginatively conceived and gracefully written. It carries the reader along with it, enlarging horizons while acknowledging problems and providing practical guidance along the way.'

Maurice Wiles, University of Oxford

www.oup.co.uk/vsi/theology